T0354077

WHAT YOUR COLLEAGUES ARE SAYING...

"Among the many resources on teaching science, this book stands out as an essential compendium of practical suggestions, thought-provoking ideas, and links to resources that support what it means for teachers and students to thrive and flourish in today's teaching and learning environment. Drawing heavily upon the wisdom of accomplished teachers and research on effective teaching and learning, this book provides much-needed guidance on navigating the complexities of today's science classrooms."

Page Keeley
Author, Speaker, and Science Education Consultant
Fort Myers, FL

"Finally, a survivor's guide to teaching! Unlike most pedagogical books, *Answers to Your Biggest Questions About Teaching Secondary Science* gives you just that—answers. From first day of school name games to year-end assessments, this educator team has brilliantly created a library of practical, implement-tomorrow structures, strategies, and tools. Cheers to a thorough teacher cheat sheet!"

Briana H. Clarke
PhET Equity and Teacher Professional Development Specialist
Oakland, CA

"This is the book science teachers have needed for a long, long time. It is both practical and profound, providing students and beginning teachers with a multifaceted vision of excellent teaching and clear strategies for progressing toward that vision. Veteran teachers will find numerous entry points to reflect on and refine their own practice, and work collaboratively with colleagues to improve education for all students."

Nicole M. Gillespie
President & CEO, The Center for Aquatic Sciences
Camden, NJ

"This is the book every science educator needs! It is organized around key questions that have the power to unlock great teaching. The authors have broad expertise and insights to offer, and they have gathered resources so that readers can easily go deeper with additional perspectives. Read it straight through or pick it up and read a section corresponding with a current dilemma—the accessible and straightforward ideas are sure to inspire."

Cynthia Passmore
Professor, School of Education, UC Davis
Davis, CA

"The only constant is change, and this book provides a tool for those trying to navigate all the new challenges teachers face in this new era of teaching. *Answers to Your Biggest Questions About Teaching Secondary Science* does a great job of acting as a roadmap for those currently in teacher training programs, new teachers, and even veteran teachers."

Chris Monsour
Instructor of Biological Science, Tiffin Columbian High School
Tiffin, OH

"If you are a beginning science teacher (or considering a change to your science classroom) and you do not know what you do not know, read this book! This book provides an insight into things you should consider about teaching science effectively that may not be covered in depth in an education program. This book is a great start to your journey in science teaching."

Anthony Tedali Stetzenmeyer
Chemistry Teacher, Knowles Teacher Initiative
Ann Arbor, MI

"This book poses concise questions that are foundational for educators to answer to achieve great science teaching. Additionally, it provides specific tips, checklists, diagrams, and resources that new and veteran educators will find invaluable for improving teaching and cultivating the joy of science with their students."

Karen Olson
Instructional Coach, Baraboo High School
2019 PAEMST National Awardee in 7–12 Science
Baraboo, WI

ANSWERS *to Your*

BIGGEST QUESTIONS *About*

TEACHING SECONDARY SCIENCE

FIVE to
THRIVE

ANSWERS *to Your*

BIGGEST QUESTIONS *About*

TEACHING SECONDARY SCIENCE

Karen Mesmer
Enya Granados
Kevin Gant
Laura Shafer
Ayanna D. Perry

For information:

Corwin
A SAGE Company
2455 Teller Road
Thousand Oaks, California 91320
(800) 233-9936
www.corwin.com

SAGE Publications Ltd.
1 Oliver's Yard
55 City Road
London, EC1Y 1SP
United Kingdom

SAGE Publications India Pvt. Ltd.
Unit No 323–333, Third Floor, F-Block
International Trade Tower Nehru Place
New Delhi – 110 019
India

SAGE Publications
Asia-Pacific Pte. Ltd.
18 Cross Street #10–10/11/12
China Square Central
Singapore 048423

Vice President and Editorial Director:
  Monica Eckman
Associate Director and Publisher,
  STEM: Erin Null
Acquisitions Editor: Debbie Hardin
Senior Editorial Assistant:
  Nyle De Leon
Production Editor: Tori Mirsadjadi
Copy Editor: Shannon Kelly
Typesetter: Integra
Proofreader: Lawrence W. Baker
Indexer: Integra
Cover Designer: Gail Buschman
Marketing Manager:
  Margaret O'Connor

Copyright © 2024 by Corwin Press, Inc.

All rights reserved. Except as permitted by U.S. copyright law, no part of this work may be reproduced or distributed in any form or by any means, or stored in a database or retrieval system, without permission in writing from the publisher.

When forms and sample documents appearing in this work are intended for reproduction, they will be marked as such. Reproduction of their use is authorized for educational use by educators, local school sites, and/or noncommercial or nonprofit entities that have purchased the book.

All third-party trademarks referenced or depicted herein are included solely for the purpose of illustration and are the property of their respective owners. Reference to these trademarks in no way indicates any relationship with, or endorsement by, the trademark owner.

Printed in the United Kingdom

Paperback ISBN 978-1-0719-1637-7

This book is printed on acid-free paper.

24 25 26 27 28 10 9 8 7 6 5 4 3 2 1

DISCLAIMER: This book may direct you to access third-party content via web links, QR codes, or other scannable technologies, which are provided for your reference by the author(s). Corwin makes no guarantee that such third-party content will be available for your use and encourages you to review the terms and conditions of such third-party content. Corwin takes no responsibility and assumes no liability for your use of any third-party content, nor does Corwin approve, sponsor, endorse, verify, or certify such third-party content.

CONTENTS

ACKNOWLEDGMENTS

We are grateful to the ideas and contributions of the many leaders, researchers, and teachers in science education that have influenced our understanding of what it means to teach science well.

Zaretta Hammond, Chris Emdin, Robin Wall Kimmerer, the JEDI committee of the National Association of Biology Teachers (NABT), Stacie Binford, Shameeka Bolton, and Ebony Omotola McGee have influenced our pursuit of equity in science teaching and learning.

You will see that works by significant science educators such as Phillip Bell, William Penuel, Brian Reiser, Cindy Passmore, James Stewart, Jennifer Cartier, Mark Windschitl, Jessica Thompson, Chris Monsour, Justin Pruneski, LeeAnn M. (Sutherland) Adams, Melissa Braaten, and many more have shaped our understanding of science teaching, modeling in the science classroom, and developing storylines that integrate science ideas and develop students' understanding of the natural world.

River Suh, Sam Long, Kirstin Milks, Brittany Franckowiak, Chris Anderson, and Megan Mosher have all influenced our thinking about gender-inclusive biology teaching.

We have relied on truly exceptional works that support teaching science content. Many are noted in the Great Resources sidebars. For example, the different editions of *5 Practices for Orchestrating Productive Task-Based Discussions in Science* (Cartier et al., 2013), *Success in Science Through Dialogue Reading and Writing* (Beauchamp et al., 2011), *Talk Science Primer* (Michaels & O'Connor, 2012), and *Ambitious Science Teaching* (Windschitl, Thompson, & Braaten, 2020) have been among our most frequently consulted resources since they were published.

And, of course, we have seen some excellent teaching in action, influenced by these research-based resources but really crafted by teachers as they worked daily to understand what worked best for their students in learning science. We've been fortunate to learn with and from teachers associated with the Knowles Teaching Initiative, National Science Teaching Association, American Modeling Teachers Association, National Association of Biology Teachers, and the Sacramento Area Science Project, BSCS Science Learning.

PUBLISHER'S ACKNOWLEDGMENTS

Corwin gratefully acknowledges the contributions of the following reviewers:

Nicole Viviane Barrie
6th/7th grade science teacher, FCUSD
Folsom, CA

Melissa Braaten
Associate professor, University of Colorado Boulder
Denver, CO

Michelle Cheyne
Adjunct faculty, Salisbury University
Cambridge, MD

Brianna Clarke
Author of *Physics4All Labs*
Oakland, CA

Kathryn Eilert
Instructional coach, Middleton High School
Middleton, WI

Deanne McClung
NBCT science teacher, science department chair, PLTW coordinator, Elkhorn Area
High School
Elkhorn, WI

Kristin Rademaker
Professional learning specialist, National Science Teaching Association

Ray Scolavino
Distinguished lecturer, UW Milwaukee
East Troy, WI

Anthony Tedaldi Stetzenmeyer
Chemistry teacher, Knowles Teacher Initiative
Ann Arbor, MI

ABOUT THE AUTHORS

Karen Mesmer, PhD, taught middle and high school science for 33 years in both northwest Alaska and in Baraboo, Wisconsin. After she retired in 2015, she started Mesmer Science Education Consulting, working as a curriculum writer, reviewer, mentor, and professional development facilitator focusing on the Next Generation Science Standards. She has been active at the local, state, and national levels in professional organizations, including serving as the president of the National Middle Level Science Teachers Association and on the board of both the National Science Teachers Association and the Wisconsin Society of Science Teachers. Karen was a recipient of the Presidential Award for Excellence in Science and Mathematics Teaching and the Ron Gibbs Award from the Wisconsin Society of Science Teachers for Lifetime Contributions to Science Education in Wisconsin. She has presented at many local, state, and national conferences. Karen was the module leader, contributor, and reviewer for Activate Learning's IQWST California Edition and a writer for the Wisconsin Science Standards as well as for four teacher guides for ONPAR assessment. She has also had articles published in *Science Scope* and two chapters in books published by the National Science Teachers Association.

Enya Granados is in her sixth year teaching as a high school life science teacher in Athens, Georgia. Enya has a passion for curriculum writing and has worked with BSCS Science Learning as a curriculum teacher co-writer on climate change. She is involved in the National Association of Biology Teachers (NABT) as an active member who presents regularly, and she chairs the organization's Justice, Equity, Diversity, and Inclusion committee. Enya was awarded the Knowles Teacher Fellowship in 2018 and NABT's Outstanding New Biology Teacher in 2021. She has published in *Teaching and Teacher Education* and for the National Center for Case Study Teaching in Science.

Kevin Gant has taught science and mathematics for 18 years, with most of his career focusing on physics education. In his most recent classroom work, he was a founder of and the lead teacher at nex+Gen Academy, a public project-based high school in Albuquerque, New Mexico. There he taught an environmental science and statistics course from 2012 to 2016. Kevin was an early adopter of project-based learning (PBL), serving as the physics teacher at New Technology High School in Napa, California, a school at the vanguard of PBL instruction. That position led to his later work at the nonprofit New Tech Network (NTN). Kevin has provided professional development and mentorship to teachers and leaders through various organizations, including the University of New Mexico, Sandia National Laboratories, and the Knowles Science Teaching Foundation. Kevin earned a B.S. in physics from the University of New Mexico, is a National Board–certified teacher (physics), and is a recipient of the Presidential Award for Excellence in Math and Science Teaching in 2015.

Laura Shafer, PhD, is a senior program officer and academy instructor for the Knowles Teacher Initiative. She taught high school physics, biology, chemistry, and integrated science, focusing on facilitating student engagement in the practices of science to develop disciplinary knowledge. She designed and implemented curriculum components for a graduate science education methods course for preservice teachers focused on supporting those teachers in developing and facilitating lessons in alignment with the Next Generation Science Standards. She provided supervision for preservice teachers developing and implementing approaches for working individually and collaboratively with resident mentor teachers. She designed and facilitated a professional development workshop series for K–12 educators, administrators, and language resource personnel to support understanding and implementation of the NGSS and integration of Common Core State Standards.

Ayanna D. Perry, PhD, is an associate director for the Teaching Fellows Program at the Knowles Teacher Initiative. She has been working in education for over 15 years. She taught high school math courses as well as college-level math education courses. In addition to her work as a teacher, she's also been working as a teacher mentor and coach for high school science and math teachers. She's published a number of blogs on issues of equity on the Knowles Teacher Initiative website and articles on technology use in math and on equity in math classes in *The Mathematics Teacher*, including "7 Features of Equitable Classroom Spaces" from her dissertation. She also co-authored *Five to Thrive: Answers to Your Biggest Questions About Teaching Secondary Math*. She is a member of the National Council of Teachers of Mathematics (NCTM), NCSM: Leadership in Mathematics Education, the Association of Mathematics Teacher Educators, the Benjamin Banneker Association, the Association of Maryland Mathematics Teacher Educators, and TODOS Mathematics for All.

INTRODUCTION

The first few years of teaching are a learning experience not only for students but also for teachers. Here are a few thoughts from us, the authors of this book:

All students are capable of making sense of the natural world.

—LAURA SHAFER, AUTHOR, TEACHER EDUCATOR, AND HIGH SCHOOL SCIENCE TEACHER

We have a lot to learn from our students and their communities.

—KEVIN GANT, AUTHOR, TEACHER EDUCATOR, HIGH SCHOOL SCIENCE TEACHER

When I started teaching, I thought I needed to have all the answers. I did not realize how much I would question what I know and what I would learn through the eyes of my students.

—AYANNA PERRY, AUTHOR, MATH AND SCIENCE TEACHER EDUCATOR, HIGH SCHOOL
MATHEMATICS TEACHER

When I started teaching, I was far away from the conveniences of running water and laboratory equipment. What I did learn was that the natural world of my remote Alaskan village was at my disposal to investigate with my students. Right outside were moose, caribou, fish, and seals that we could study, monitoring their populations using information from locals who live off the land.

We could go out the front door of the school and see what the waves from a storm had done to the environment. This was very different from my personal reality of what it means to learn science and how to teach science. I now know it's important to take into consideration your surroundings, the students you teach, their culture, and the resources that you have.

—**KAREN MESMER,** AUTHOR AND 6–12 SCIENCE TEACHER

All students deserve good science teachers.

—**ENYA GRANADOS,** AUTHOR AND HIGH SCHOOL LIFE SCIENCE TEACHER

You may be surprised by what you thought you knew about teaching and what you come to understand after only a few years in the classroom. This is true even for those of us who have been teaching for a while, because each year you teach, your experiences will help your craft evolve. As you progress, you will learn more about how to connect with your students and how to support their growing identities as learners of science. You will be amazed by how much your understanding of topics you thought you knew well deepens because of the questions and ideas put forth by your students. This book shares the things we've learned from our students and our teaching that have helped us improve our practice.

WHY IS TEACHING SCIENCE DIFFERENT TODAY?

In the last two decades we have seen an abrupt paradigm shift in science education, a move away from procedural lab investigations and direct instruction and toward increased emphasis on reasoning, sense-making, phenomena exploration, problem-solving, and collaboration. Science education reform has happened in some areas around the country, but many classrooms still rely on a fairly traditional notion of science learning. The most prominent call to reform science education in the past two decades has come in the form of the Next Generation Science Standards (NGSS). The NGSS address the commitment to position-developing explanatory knowledge by integrating three dimensions:

1   Science and Engineering Practices (SEPs),
2   Disciplinary Core Ideas (DCIs),
3   Crosscutting Concepts (CCCs) (National Research Council, 2012).

These three dimensions are integrated so that students build an understanding of the DCIs by engaging in the science practices while also recognizing the CCCs within and across science disciplines. Teaching and learning as envisioned by the NGSS represents a dramatic departure from approaches to teaching and learning that occur in many science classrooms (Banilower et al., 2013).

Rather than supporting students to learn *about* science, these guiding documents ask teachers to support students to *figure out* science. Figuring out science is what allows students to *do* science actively rather than receive instruction passively. New educators that are coming into the fold have developed their identity as doers of science. In response to meeting the goal for teaching and learning envisioned by the NGSS, they need some additional and accessible grounding to understand what looks different from the way they learned science. They also need to understand why the new teaching method is important and how it supports all of the children in their care to become capable learners and doers of science. Given that the NGSS standards are fairly complex, teachers need a simple way to understand what teaching this way looks like in practice.

WHAT EXACTLY *IS* DIFFERENT ABOUT TEACHING AND LEARNING SCIENCE TODAY?

This shift from knowing about science ideas to figuring out and reasoning with science ideas is at odds with the traditional way of teaching science. The ways of teaching championed by this book aim to increase the likelihood that students will develop deep understanding. This will afford them the opportunity to reason about questions they have about how the natural world works.

Science Then	Science Now
Learning about: • Students memorize facts, formulas, cycles, and vocabulary. • Teachers present information to the entire class and students replicate models.	Figuring out: • Students apply prior knowledge to reason with and build disciplinary core ideas. • Teachers present phenomena to explore. Students work in groups to develop and revise models to explain scientific phenomena.
Working alone	Working collaboratively
Teachers design investigations that confirm the answer or concept introduced. • Teachers design cookbook labs where all the directions are laid out for students. • Access to investigations is a reward for compliance. A privilege for honors and high-level classes.	Students plan and carry out investigations to start the learning. • Students figure out the answer or develop an idea by carrying out an investigation. • All students can investigate. • Prescriptive lab investigations can be used to build and develop facility with laboratory equipment and promote safe engagement in the lab.
Scientists are smart (and all look like Albert Einstein). There are science people.	Everyone is capable of doing science and engaging in sense-making.
Science happens in the laboratory. • Learning happens in the physical classroom.	Science happens everywhere, including a science laboratory and the natural world. • Learning happens outside of the classroom with community stakeholders.
Hypothetical scenarios drive instruction.	Natural phenomena drive instruction.

Science Then	Science Now
Science disciplines are isolated topics. • Content is disconnected.	Crosscutting concepts and science and engineering practices are used to teach interdisciplinary approaches to science. • Integrated storylines mean more than one science discipline is used to explain a phenomenon.
Students use worksheets, read textbooks, and answer questions at the end of the chapter to demonstrate understanding.	Students create journal articles, posters, and media presentations based on their research to demonstrate understanding.

HOW DOES THIS BOOK HELP?

This book is based on our years in education, as classroom teachers, science coaches, department chairs, and professional development providers and creators. We have spent our careers as learners, privileged to learn by taking courses, engaging with colleagues, teaching, engaging in our own classroom inquiry, doing research in classrooms, and reading the work published by trusted members of the field. The questions this book poses are from our own experience and from what the teachers we work with ask. Our answers are based on our experience, practice, and research. The book is organized into five categories framed by overarching questions:

1. How do I build a positive science community?
2. How do I structure, organize, and manage my science class?
3. How do I engage my students in science?
4. How do I help my students talk about science?
5. How do I know what my students know and how can I use that information to plan and move them forward?

Interspersed throughout the book are sidebar notes on fostering identity and agency, access and equity, teaching in flexible settings, and related great resources for deeper learning. This book is not an in-depth look at any of these topics. There are fantastic resources that cover each of our topics in more depth, many of which are mentioned in the Great Resources sidebars and our list of references at the back of the book. We wrote this book to be easy to read and to provide reliable and practical guidance as you work to improve your craft as a teacher. We acknowledge that teaching a secondary science course is different from many other subjects because there are strands/disciplines in science that in some ways overlap and in other ways are unique. When there is overlap we work to be explicit about that, and when the applications of this knowledge show up in unique ways across the different courses, we work to make that clear as well.

Science is a unique discipline with norms and practices. Teaching science is an endeavor where you keep learning more over the years. You try out new things, modify, collaborate with others, and add to your practice as you gain experience.

—HIGH SCHOOL SCIENCE TEACHER

WHO IS THIS BOOK FOR?

This book is for preservice teachers, in-service teachers, administrators, coaches, professional development providers, and educators who support the teaching of science in secondary classrooms. Preservice teachers can use this text as a way to focus their reflections when they are observing classes and as an aid when they start their own student teaching. In-service teachers, beginning or experienced, can use it to learn more about implementing current practices in science education that they have not had the time to research or consider using in their classrooms. They can also use the book to get ideas about teaching a different science course than the one they are familiar with. In addition, this book might offer in-service teachers ideas about trying something new, such as setting common classroom norms or reframing the need for class notes. Using this book helps to make all of these tasks more manageable.

Administrators can use this book to support them in conducting classroom observations and giving targeted feedback to their science teachers. The book can assist administrators in deepening their knowledge of best practices for teaching science. Teacher coaches, including university supervisors, district-level content coaches, and cooperating teachers, can use this book to help them in providing feedback and strategies to the teachers they are supporting. Professional development providers, methods course instructors, and other members of the schools of education might use this as a supplementary text in their courses or mention it to new teachers as a just-in-time resource to support their future instruction. This book is useful for providing specific guidance on how to implement effective science teaching practices for the teachers they work with.

In addition, special education teachers, teachers of multilingual students, paraeducators, and those who co-teach or support science education can use this book to learn more about providing differentiation and support in science classes and about building learning communities. The structure of this text makes it useful for one-on-one conversations, grade-level meetings, and district-level meetings, and it also provides a practical basis for classroom walk-bys and observations because of the focus on effective teaching practices in bite-sized chunks.

HOW CAN YOU USE THIS BOOK?

In the foreword of *5 Practices for Orchestrating Productive Task-Based Discussions in Science* (Cartier et al., 2013), Mark Windschitl suggests that for teachers to grow professionally, they need to prioritize working with colleagues, be in a school where administration believe in and support that collaboration, and have available the appropriate tools to develop a shared vision for and support of their work and outcomes. This book is designed to contribute to the set of ideas that you might discuss with your colleagues. It is written in a way where you can learn about a range of approaches for advancing your practice in a particular area.

For example, the questions that contribute to learning how to build a positive science community are:

- How do I build a positive scientific community in my classroom?
- How do I help cultivate a sense of the wonder, joy, and beauty of science?
- What is equity in a science learning community?
- How do I learn about my students' identities?

- How do I support student agency in my classroom?
- How can I dislodge negative narratives students carry about their science identities?
- How do I establish two-way communication with caregivers?

This book also supports you in gaining targeted knowledge on a singular topic, like "What is the role of student notes?" (see Chapter 5). We believe that teachers are most fulfilled when they can direct their own professional learning, and we see this text as a support for that. This book is useful for answering questions that you have about your practice and the practices of others, gaining new ideas or strategies for growing your teacher toolbox, and inviting colleagues into conversations about what it means to teach in a way that centers students.

Centering students means eliciting their prior knowledge, inviting them to share about their identity, providing a range of ways for them to engage authentically in the content, and drawing on the wealth of knowledge gained from colleagues and other school staff to support them.

Other useful ways to engage with this text include doing a scan of the table of contents and choosing questions to review during the year for your own professional development or doing a read-through at the beginning of the year to note ideas that you want to try during the year. However you choose to engage with the myriad ideas in this book, we hope you will

- pace yourself;
- know that it takes time to change practice;
- understand we learn most from practice, reflection, and collaborative inquiry; and
- know that the first try of a new strategy can be a challenge.

There is a list of resources at the end of this book to support your continued growth. Review these resources to find content and community as you continue to grow as a teacher. Becoming the best science teacher that you can involves an experiment where hypotheses are tested and outcomes described. The end goal is continuing to develop a working model of teaching that reflects your context, students, and beliefs.

HOW DO I BUILD A POSITIVE SCIENCE COMMUNITY?

- -

This chapter offers strategies for creating the science community you envision for your classroom. Making your classroom into a community of learners who are encouraged to work together to investigate, develop, revise, and share the ideas that are the target of your instruction takes time and requires you, your students, and your students' families to work together. Building a positive community helps your students experience success and feel that they are capable doers of science. One important aspect of your community is how you position your students as authors of ideas and sense makers in your classroom. This chapter points you to ways you can support students in developing a positive science identity and exercising student agency in the classroom.

Another aspect of your classroom community is how students will interact with one another. The norms you establish play an important role because they guide student interactions and directly impact how students will communicate with each other. This chapter offers support in developing and maintaining classroom norms.

Your science community extends beyond the walls of your classroom as it engages families to partner in the work of supporting students' learning. We use the word *caregivers* to reflect the diverse circumstances each student brings to the classroom. Establishing two-way communication with caregivers is one of the best ways to support your students' learning.

It is very important to ensure your classroom is a safe space for each student. A sense of safety and belonging encourages students to share ideas and support each other in respectful ways. Sharing the beauty and wonder of science and fostering curiosity and excitement about figuring out how the natural world works are important catalysts to prompt students to share ideas and questions with one another. When they share, they are helping each other to figure out science and not just learn about it.

This chapter helps you to create and maintain a positive science community by providing answers to the following questions:

- ☐ **What are some ways to build a positive scientific community?**
- ☐ **How do I help cultivate a sense of the wonder, joy, and beauty of science?**
- ☐ **What is equity in a science learning community?**
- ☐ **How do I learn about my students' identities?**
- ☐ **How do I support student agency in my classroom?**
- ☐ **How can I dislodge the negative narratives my students carry about their science identities?**
- ☐ **How do I establish two-way communication with caregivers?**

As you read about each of these topics, we encourage you to reflect on the following questions:

- ☐ **What does this mean to me?**
- ☐ **What else do I need to know about this?**
- ☐ **What will I do next?**

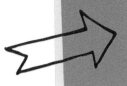

What Are Some Ways to Build a Positive Scientific Community?

Students will learn science when they feel safe, capable, and supported in their classroom. Learning how to build this type of classroom community and sustain it will help you support your students' science learning. It provides a way to build trust within the classroom so that students can work together to figure out science ideas and solve problems.

Tip 1 | Know your students; let them know you and each other too

A positive science community begins with building positive relationships with your students. Positive relationships start with getting to know your students (see Identities p. 21) and providing ways for your students to get to know you and each other.

Tip 2 | Model the behavior you expect

Developing norms and modeling them helps you and your students create and protect positivity in your classroom (see Norms p. 71; Routines p. 64). To students, there is nothing as jarring as being surprised in front of their classmates. Students feel safe and are able to contribute to the classroom when they understand what is expected of them. Consistent and positive feedback about interactions in the classroom helps reinforce positive interactions. Sometimes this requires you to be both firm and friendly. Students do not need an adult friend who is "just like them." Rather, students need someone who can model positive learning stances and facilitate their learning in ways that emphasize how your norms are contributing to an equitable learning environment.

Tip 3 | Create a welcoming atmosphere

Think about what you want students to see and feel when they walk into their classroom (see Start of the Year p. 34):

- How will you arrange your classroom?
- How does your classroom space allow for community interactions?
- Do you have easy access to all groups?
- Do your students have a way to visit other groups to share ideas?
- What could be on your walls?
- How are you providing your students with examples that promote an inclusive learning environment?

Hang motivational posters about thinking in ways that celebrate the twists and turns of building and revising ideas (see Productive Struggle p. 100) and that showcase scientists from a variety of ethnic, gender, and social backgrounds (see Start of the Year p. 34). Celebrate students by displaying student work that exemplifies the different steps in problem-solving and celebrates the important mistakes along the way (see Productive Struggle p. 100; Agency p. 23). Post procedures and routines (see Start of the Year p. 34).

I have the list of procedures posted on the wall to remind students about them. When they ask me a question about a procedure, I point to the list and they then know what to do. I am not ignoring their request. I am supporting them in using the resources we have in the classroom.

–HIGH SCHOOL PHYSICS TEACHER

HOW DO I SUSTAIN A POSITIVE SCIENTIFIC COMMUNITY?

A positive community makes the hard work of students working together and sharing ideas easier for everyone. It takes work from you and from your students to nurture and grow a positive science community. A key part of this process is continuing to build relationships and to revisit the norms that are supporting your classroom. Make it a point to revisit relationship building throughout the year and make learning about your students a regular routine (see Identities p. 21). Ask regularly for student input about the ways the norms are working for them (see Norms p. 71). Have regular community check-ins with your students. Listen to what your students are saying about their participation in your class. Have students reflect on the ways they are or are not experiencing a positive community and revise as needed. If the class is not working with a shared vision about how you will interact when learning, it will be difficult to meet your goals for a positive scientific community.

This table details goals for building an inclusive community, what to do, and what not to do to help you sustain a positive science community in your classroom.

Goal	What to Do	What Not to Do
Every student is part of the science thinking in the class.	Establish routines and grouping for solving problems that provide individual think time, group time, and sharing out (see Talk Formats p. 120).	If the goal is to help students figure out and make sense of science, do not employ an "I do, we do, you do" classroom routine. There are times when this strategy is appropriate, however, such as when teaching lab safety.
Foster and build a growth mindset.	Model your high expectations for student thinking and share your belief that all students can attain your goals.	Do not give tasks that are easily accomplished or explain where you anticipate they will struggle (see Productive Struggle p. 100). Students grow when they productively struggle.
We learn from our mistakes.	Ask students why they chose an explanation and ask further questions to have them see any inconsistencies in their answer. This helps students to understand that they can learn and grow from an error. It's okay to not have a completely correct and/or complete answer at the beginning.	Do not only share correct answers. This indicates to students that they should focus on getting the correct answer and not on learning and growing from an incorrect or incomplete answer.

(Continued)

(Continued)

Goal	What to Do	What Not to Do
Every student is important to the class.	Share different solution pathways for a task. Make connections among students' work and highlight their contributions to the task. Share many students' work with the entire class in order to show that everyone is important.	Do not share one solution only. Do not let one group's work speak for the entire class.
Students are responsible members of a learning community.	Highlight when you see positive behaviors: "I noticed several groups are sharing their methods with each other." Talk with students who are not following the norms one-on-one or with as much privacy as possible.	Do not call out a student publicly for not following a norm. Do not impose classroom restrictions for all students when norms aren't followed by a few. You may want to consider imposing consequences on those that are not following norms, especially if safety issues are involved.

Notes

How Do I Help Cultivate a Sense of the Wonder, Joy, and Beauty of Science?

A Framework for Science Education (National Research Council, 2012) outlined a vision and laid the groundwork for the writing of the NGSS. Early in the text the authors wrote,

> *The overarching goal of our framework for K–12 science education is to ensure that by the end of 12th grade, all students have some appreciation of the beauty and wonder of science; possess sufficient knowledge of science and engineering to engage in public discussions on related issues; are careful consumers of scientific and technological information related to their everyday lives; are able to continue to learn about science outside school; and have the skills to enter careers of their choice, including (but not limited to) careers in science, engineering, and technology. (National Research Council, 2012, p. 1)*

It is significant that ensuring all students have some appreciation of the beauty and wonder of science is the first thing mentioned. Images from the James Webb Space Telescope can fascinate students by showing them what is far away in our universe. Alternatively, examining cells under a microscope opens students' minds to the life processes happening in our cells that work together to keep us alive. Shifting science instruction from memorizing facts to seeing astounding things, big and small, that are both breathtaking and relevant to their lives can help students focus on the wonder around them that science strives to explain.

HOW CAN I USE STORIES TO HELP MY STUDENTS APPRECIATE THE WONDER OF SCIENCE?

Teaching science using phenomena in a storyline approach helps students to appreciate the wonder of science (see Unit Planning p. 56). Here are some tips to get you started in your classroom.

Tip 1   Start a unit with an observable, natural event

A local phenomenon is preferable if possible since it helps students see the relevance to their lives. Ask students what they notice and what they wonder. This can be as simple as having students fill out a Notice and Wonder Chart.

What do I notice?	What do I wonder?

Student questions guide the investigations that are needed to figure out how the phenomenon works. Using this approach, students are doing the wondering and not just filling out answers on a worksheet about the steps in the Krebs cycle, or converting a page of chemical formulas to their chemical name. Exercises like these do not encourage wonder in students and can instead kill their enthusiasm for science.

Great Resources

These two resources give more information about how to encourage students to ask questions:

- Wonder and Notice Protocol, https://bit.ly/4443w04
- The Question Formulation Technique, https://bit.ly/3jjkwyn

Tip 2 Have students plan and conduct investigations into questions without knowing the answer before they start

In this way they can experience wonder and joy about figuring out how things work. Sharing their models and explanations and arguing about them aid in the endeavor of making science fun and exciting.

HOW CAN WE SHOW STUDENTS THE BEAUTY OF NATURE?

Great Resources

Check out The Wonder of Science at https://thewonderofscience.com/, the homepage of which proclaims "Don't kill the wonder."

Taking students outside can help them see the wonder and beauty in nature. They can observe and ask questions about how birds fly and learn about small organisms that live in the soil. Making sense of how organisms transform energy and cycle matter shows them how biology, chemistry, and physics are interwoven in the real world. A sense of beauty emerges about how things in our world, both very large and very small, work together and connect. Science is everywhere, and being outside makes that real to students. They can be instilled with a sense of awe and wonder at how things in the world work together.

> I feel wonder when I am out in nature. My seventh-grade science teacher instilled this sense of wonder in me when he took me outside during class and on field trips. I became fascinated with how our natural world works and spent my 34-year career as a wildlife biologist helping to figure out the population ecology of many fur-bearing animals.
>
> —WILDLIFE BIOLOGIST

WHAT OTHER RESOURCES ARE AVAILABLE THAT WILL HELP ME ILLUSTRATE THE WONDER OF SCIENCE TO MY STUDENTS?

Stories of scientists in text or video can show students how science can elicit wonder. Many scientists see their work as a form of play and continue in their chosen field long past retirement age. They see beauty in the phenomena they chose to study. Science can be likened to a jigsaw puzzle scientists assemble, and when a picture emerges, they get a deep sense of satisfaction and joy. What happens in the brain when scientists solve a puzzle is very similar to when we hear musical harmony and feel a sense of joy (Owens, 2022, p. 1).

People do jigsaw puzzles for fun and scientists often view their work in this same light.

Great Resources

Oases of Life by@AusAntarctic Science TV, https://bit.ly/3JuOwRQ; This Is What a Scientist Looks Like, https://bit.ly/3qXyQjs.

COMMUNITY

Source: iStock.com/Francesco Scatena

They play with ideas and equipment in labs, and some go out in the wild to collect data on populations or organisms and have fun as they are doing it. Teachers need to make sure that students have the same opportunity to find beauty in doing science.

Here are some books with stories of scientists who had a sense for the wonder, joy, and beauty of science. Students may benefit by reading some of these to understand how practicing scientists view their work.

● Archibald, G. (2016). *My life with cranes*. International Crane Foundation.

● Barres, B. (2020). *The autobiography of a transgender scientist*. MIT Press.

● Fausch, K. D. (2015). *For the love of rivers: A scientist's journey*. Oregon State University Press.

● Harrington, J. N. (2019). *Buzzing with questions: The inquisitive mind of Charles Henry Turner*. Illustrated by T. Taylor III. Calkins Creek.

● Jahren, H. (2016). *Lab girl*. Knopf.

● Keating, J. (2017). *Shark lady: The true story of how Eugenie Clark became the ocean's most fearless scientist*. Illustrated by Marta Álvarez Miguéns. Sourcebooks, Inc.

● Keller, E. F. (1984). *A feeling for the organism: The life and work of Barbara McClintock* (10th anniversary ed.). Macmillan.

● Kimmerer, R. W. (2022). *Braiding sweetgrass: Indigenous wisdom, scientific knowledge, and the teaching of plants*. Zest Books.

● Lanham, J. D. (2016). *The home place: Memoirs of a colored man's love affair with nature*. Milkweed Editions.

● Shetterly, M. L. (2016). *Hidden figures: The American Dream and the untold story of the Black women mathematicians who helped win the space race*. William Morrow.

● Wilson, E. O. (1994). *Naturalist*. Island Press.

HOW MIGHT STARTING A SCIENCE CLUB INTRODUCE THE JOY OF SCIENCE TO MY STUDENTS?

A science club can be a good way to get students involved in science in a way that encourages them to think about its relevance in their own lives. Here are some tips for success.

Tip 1 You might want to start with an established science activity, such as Science Olympiad, Exploravision, the National Association of Biology Teachers BioClub, or eCybermission

Great Resources

For more information about each of these opportunities, visit the websites below:

- Science Olympiad, https://www.soinc.org/

- Exploravision, https://www.exploravision.org/

- National Association of Biology Teachers BioClub, https://bit.ly/318Eaqk

- eCybermission, https://www.ecybermission.com/

Tip 2 Activities for a science club could be field trips, presentations by people with a science-related career, or projects such as helping with local land management

WHO CAN DO SCIENCE?

The resounding answer to this question is that *anyone* can do science! Your attitude about science and who can do science can contribute to cultivating a sense of the wonder, joy, and beauty of science (see Identities p. 21).

Here are some summarizing tips about cultivating a sense of wonder and joy about science.

Tip 1 *Be excited about what you are helping students to discover and provide opportunities where they see science as a way to make sense of the natural world, not just as a body of knowledge to be memorized*

There is wonder, joy, and beauty to be found as students figure out how a magnetic cannon works, how moon phases happen, and how a tree can grow so tall.

Tip 2 *Be supportive of all students learning science and becoming scientists*

This will add to the sense of a science community and make the whole process both more equitable and more fun for everyone.

Access and Equity

Students can feel a sense of belonging in a club that is focused on science and through experiencing things that they may not be exposed to during a science class. For example, they could be involved in removing invasive species in a prairie or woodland. If funding is an issue, consider platforms like DonorsChoose to fund these opportunities for students.

COMMUNITY

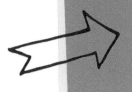

What Is Equity in a Science Learning Community?

We all carry frameworks and beliefs that inform our science teaching. These include our values, perspectives, and lived experiences. Students also carry these frameworks and beliefs with them about what science is and who can do science. Equity is one of the most important frameworks to consider when teaching. In this section we will define equity, explain why it's important, and share resources to support you in being an equitable science educator.

WHAT IS THE DIFFERENCE BETWEEN EQUALITY AND EQUITY?

Equity and *equality* are two terms that are often used interchangeably, but they mean very different things. Equality in education means giving all of the students the same things (same materials, same instruction, same everything). In contrast, equity means giving all of the students *what they need*, which means different students get different materials, instruction, etc., in support of learning the same science. This distinction is important because no two students are the same. Each comes to your classroom with very different needs, thus it is important that your teaching meets these different student needs.

Parent and Child Cooking	Able-Bodied Person Cooking	Wheelchair User in the Kitchen

Source: iStock.com/ Monkeybusinessimages	*Source*: iStock.com/Lyndon Stratford/istock.com	*Source*: iStock.com/AnnaStills

When learning to cook in a kitchen in an equal context, everyone receives the same materials (same height of counter, same cooking utensils, etc). In an equitable context everyone receives different materials according to their needs (changing the counter height, variety of cooking utensils, etc.).

WHY IS EQUITY IN SCIENCE TEACHING IMPORTANT?

Inequities currently exist in our education system. You might see this in school funding, racial/ethnic representation disparities, economic disparities, disparities with regards to students with diverse abilities, and more.

One such example can be observed in tracked classes. Tracking is the practice of placing students in classes based on their achievement in prior coursework or on exams, or through estimations of a student's ability. This can take the form of honors versus on-level courses, or recommending all students who don't achieve over a certain grade in one class be shifted to a lower-level course next. Oftentimes these classes have differences in representation with regards to gender, race and ethnicity, and ability, with privileged identities being more represented in higher-level coursework.

We also see these disparities present in the fields of science. Science has a history of marginalizing particular groups of people and using science to further marginalize them, especially when marginalized identities intersect (e.g., the Tuskegee syphilis studies, Henrietta Lacks's stolen cells, the eugenic sterilization of women of color and with disabilities, the pathologization of queerness).

Great Resources

- *Black, Brown, Bruised: How Racialized STEM Education Stifles Innovation* by Ebony Omotola McGee

- *Why Is Tracking Harmful?* https://bit.ly/3XqrvVJ

- *We Want to Do More Than Survive: Abolitionist Teaching and the Pursuit of Educational Freedom* by Bettina Love

Because these inequities exist, it is important for you as a teacher to practice equitable teaching in your classroom. Equitable teaching leads to

- creative problem-solving due to diverse perspectives,
- stronger collaboration and understanding of one another,
- a more empathetic environment,
- a society that is better able to care for itself.

WHAT DOES EQUITY IN SCIENCE TEACHING LOOK LIKE?

Equity in science teaching looks like:

1. **Believing that all students can learn and do science.**
   a   All students have access to opportunities to learn through cognitively demanding tasks.
   b   All students are held to high expectations.
   c   All students are heard.

2. **Valuing diversity in everything.** There is diversity in . . .
   a   the ways for students to engage in science (see Practices p. 48),
   b   the approaches to teach science,
   c   the ways students talk about science (see Talk Formats p. 120; Facilitation p. 124),
   d   the structures of science activities,
   e   the representation of scientists,

Access and Equity

Intersectionality is a framework that helps us understand how multiple identities combine to create experiences of marginalization or privilege. This framework can be useful in 1) reflecting on your own experiences of advantages and disadvantages, 2) understanding your students' experiences, 3) identifying perspectives present or absent in your curriculum, and 4) recognizing the differential impacts science has on society and people. You can learn more about its origin from Dr. Kimberlé Crenshaw in her TED talk, "The Urgency of Intersectionality."

f the epistemologies (frameworks of what we know and how we know these things) of science (western science, indigenous science, etc.),

g students' backgrounds, experiences, and thoughts (see Identities p. 21).

3   **Identifying the systemic structures and practices that marginalize students.** Grading policies, type and frequency of summative assessments, and tracking are all systemic structures that might marginalize some of your learners. Asking students how these policies or practices impact them is one way to learn about harmful policies that you and your colleagues might push to change.

> *I noticed that there was a lot of variety in our grading practices as a department and some seemed problematic to my values. I found myself reflecting and asking questions about our school's grading policies and whether or not they were equitable. Are we holding students to high standards? Do our grading policies reflect that? What does equitable grading look like? When is it ok to be flexible and when is it not?*
>
> **−VIRTUAL HIGH SCHOOL LIFE SCIENCE TEACHER**

4   **Embracing the process.** There is no linear path to being an equitable science educator and no end goal. We are always learning and growing through reflection, collaboration, and education.

    a Reflect on your own experiences in the sciences.

        i How do you see yourself and your community in science?

        ii Do you believe that you, people in your community, and people of your gender have contributed to the ways that science has shaped the current world? Are there examples that you can readily share?

        iii How did you learn and engage in science?

    b Reflect on the perspectives missing in science and the cultural situatedness of science and science learning.

5   **Recentering science learning as culturally relevant and based on students interests.** (See Culturally Relevant p. 52.)
Students engage in doing science when units and lessons are planned with their interests and cultures in mind. It also helps to have multiple and diverse representations and local, relevant phenomena.

6   **Acknowledging the ethical, moral, and cultural impacts of science.** The findings of science are not separate from how those findings influence us ethically, morally, and culturally. It is helpful to students if those effects on us are brought into the classroom (see Culturally Relevant p. 52).

Great Resources

- STEM teaching tool on promoting equity in science education, https://bit.ly/3pgh5LT
- Gender-inclusive framework, https://bit.ly/3OFwvD4
- Guide to using gender-inclusive language, https://bit.ly/44fPVDO
- *Trans Studies in K–12 Education: Creating an Agenda for Research and Practice,* edited by Mario I. Suarez and Melinda M. Mangin
- *Braiding Sweetgrass: Indigenous Wisdom, Scientific Knowledge, and the Teaching of Plants* by Robin Wall Kimmerer

Access and Equity

Discuss with your co-teachers (ESOL, SPED, and paraprofessionals) what it means to teach equitably; their training will have provided them some valuable perspectives and expertise.

How Do I Learn About My Students' Identities?

Students are more than just science learners with science identities; they have passions, families, friends, concerns, and more that exist outside of your classroom. Although you are not in control of most things beyond your classroom, welcoming students' full identities and experiences into the classroom in both your science instruction and general demeanor are important for engaging students. If you get to know them, their identities can be assets to your classroom teaching.

HOW COULD I PRIORITIZE LEARNING ABOUT STUDENTS' IDENTITIES AS A REGULAR ROUTINE?

Whether you choose simple written activities like surveys or organize entire community culture days, plan for a variety of opportunities to have conversations with students. These activities can relate to the science content directly or just focus on getting to know one another. Here are some examples of routines to help prioritize learning about student identity:

- A daily routine could be as simple as greeting students by name at the door or asking questions about your students in a bell ringer.
- A weekly routine might include celebrating events in students' lives every Monday or dedicating time for students to share what they are thankful for every Friday.
- A monthly routine might include a significant portion of class time dedicated to reflecting on class norms, structured socializing, a monthly program (e.g., Black Lives Matter at School Week), or any other larger topic that would meet the needs of students at school.

HOW DO I DEVELOP CULTURAL COMPETENCE?

Cultural competence is the ability of an individual to learn about one's own culture and other cultures (Hammond, 2014). As a teacher, you can reflect on your own cultural identity and provide spaces for students to do so as well. After reflection, opportunities for students to understand one another's cultures can happen during science content teaching, when studying various perspectives on any given phenomena or problem, or even just when getting to know one another in the classroom.

Tip 1 | Cultures are not monolithic

Students have a variety of cultures that they identify with. It is not appropriate for you to assume what it looks like or means to a student to identify with a particular culture. Take the time to learn more about your students' relationships with their cultures.

One possible activity is multicultural bags:

1. Have students decorate paper bags with their names, a favorite quote/lyric, and symbols that represent their identities.
2. Inside of their bag students include information like their learning philosophy, how they see themselves as a science student, their greatest fear, their

Teaching in Flexible Settings

There are a variety of resources to engage students in virtual contexts. For individual sharing, Google Forms and Pear Decks are a great way to see student responses. For group sharing, Nearpod, Jamboard, and Padlet are helpful platforms for students to see one another's perspectives synchronously or asynchronously.

greatest passion, the greatest risk they have ever taken, their hero, something no one in the class knows about them, and anything else they would like to share.

3   In addition to whatever else they want to share, all students include the same information on two strips of paper: one thing they need from the class and one thing they can give to the class.

4   Students share their bags in a circle as a way to get to know one another. Don't forget to make one for yourself to share too!

5   Display the bags so that student work and identities can become an integral part of classroom decorations.

I teach in a context where I serve a lot of international students. Students are much more likely to learn when they know that you love and care about them first and affirm their multiple cultures. At the beginning of the year, I have students make "multicultural" bags and share about themselves with the entire class so that we can learn more about one another.

–HIGH SCHOOL LIFE SCIENCE TEACHER

HOW CAN I EMBED GETTING TO KNOW STUDENTS' PERSPECTIVES AND IDENTITIES WITHIN COURSEWORK?

Many of the phenomena and solutions discussed in a lesson or unit can have a variety of perspectives as to how they might impact individuals with different identities. Embedding opportunities for students to share their perspectives on class content and tie it back to their identities can be affirming to them as knowledge creators and make coursework relevant to their lives. This can be done within a class activity or through exit tickets, class discussions, bell ringers, or homework (see Culturally Relevant p. 52 for more).

HOW COULD I SUPPORT STUDENTS' INTERESTS RELEVANT TO THEIR IDENTITIES?

Taking time to get to know students' interests and then supporting them can be meaningful for students. This could be showing up at community events (that are school based or not), coaching a sport, volunteering as a club advisor at the school, or connecting students to opportunities outside of school.

Notes

How Do I Support Student Agency in My Classroom?

Student agency is defined as the choice and control students have about the decisions and contributions they make in the classroom. Research has shown that students who have agency in their learning have improved engagement in science practices (Holmes et al., 2020), are more motivated, and experience greater satisfaction in their learning (Lin-Siegler et al., 2016). Having a plan for how you will assist students in exercising agency in the science classroom is an important step in supporting your students' engagement in science practices.

IN WHAT WAYS CAN STUDENTS EXERCISE AGENCY?

Science is guided by a series of decisions scientists make about the knowledge developed through and grounded in the practices of science. Likewise, engaging students in scientific practices (see Practices p. 48) requires students to make decisions about the knowledge they are generating at different points in their learning trajectories. To make successful decisions in support of a learning goal, students need an opportunity to be co-owners of their learning space. Developing a space where students feel able to direct how they engage in the classroom requires student agency.

Here are some tips to guide you in increasing student agency in your classroom.

Tip 1 Ask for student feedback on their participation in activities or their thoughts about class structures; this gives you an insight into student preferences

- Include regular checkpoints in your lessons to learn whether your planned approach to the work is supporting student learning. Consider whether students need to change groups, have more independent thinking time, want to share their ideas with other groups or the class for feedback, etc. As you teach, look for times when you can invite student choice that could improve how students engage and support your learning goals.

> I ask students for feedback all the time around a variety of different things that range from grouping choices, the time needed for review, and how they like to review. Getting these formative pulse checks helps me assess my teaching and their growth as well.
>
> **–NINTH-GRADE ENVIRONMENTAL SCIENCE TEACHER**

Tip 2 | Promote and support student choice when engaging in science practices

For example:

Great Resources

Using the Question Formulation Technique provides students agency over which question they want to investigate in a supported way. Learn about it at https://rightquestion.org/what-is-the-qft/.

- Asking questions: Provide students an opportunity to brainstorm questions about a phenomenon and have students choose a question to investigate.
- Planning and carrying out investigations: Provide students with materials and let them choose which ones they will use and how they will design their investigation.
- Developing and using models: Provide opportunities for students to decide how they will represent parts of their model and how they will illustrate the different ways those parts interact over time.
- Constructing explanations: Provide multiple format choices for constructing an explanation (see Technology p. 103).

> While writing is an important platform for communicating in science, I also offer other ways for students to share their explanations. Some of my most detailed explanations have come from students creating videos with Flip.
>
> **—ELEVENTH-GRADE CONCEPTUAL PHYSICS TEACHER**

Great Resources

These resources provide a bank of phenomena choices and their alignment with DCIs: https://www.ngssphenomena.com/; https://thewonderofscience.com/phenomenal; https://ngss.sdcoe.net/Phenomena-and-the-NGSS/-ProjectPhenomena-Database.

Tip 3 | Give students more ownership of portions of the lesson

- One way to provide students with agency is to give them the choice of what tasks they will engage in. For example, there are many different phenomena that are useful in helping students to build a specific DCI. Providing a range of choices as to which phenomena to investigate is one way to give students choice and ownership in a part of your lesson.

Tip 4 | Let students choose what work to display on the classroom walls

- Often teachers choose the work displayed on classroom walls. Featuring student work that students have selected in a public and conspicuous place illustrates to others that ideas are celebrated and shared in your classroom. When student ideas are made public, this can lead to students developing a positive science identity because everyone will be seen as capable doers of science and as having worthwhile ideas to contribute.
- Dedicate a wall space for student work that students want to post. Provide a space for students to share why this work was important to them.
- Dedicate a wall space for initial model ideas. This sends a message that all initial contributions are important in coming to a consensus on the final model.
- Dedicate a wall space for the best mistakes. These are mistakes that help us focus our understanding and make informed decisions about our next steps (see Productive Struggle p. 100).
- Rotate posted work regularly so that all students have a chance to share.

How Can I Dislodge Negative Narratives My Students Carry About Their Science Identities?

Students' beliefs about their ability to do science greatly impacts their engagement with a science class (Kim et al., 2018), so working to dislodge any negative misconceptions they have about themselves is important.

Here are some tips about how to reframe students' conceptions of themselves and their ability to do science.

Tip 1 Provide constant feedback

Giving students feedback regularly both on formal assignments and informally while completing tasks in class can give students clarity and confidence in their science skills and abilities (see Feedback p. 142). Addressing comments like "I'm just not a science student" or "I'm not good at science" immediately is a great opportunity to reframe and challenge students' thinking of their own abilities.

Tip 2 Include opportunities for reflection

Provide students space and time to reflect on what they are learning in class and on their own scientific identities. Regularly include reflection prompts and class discussions of how they are engaging in the scientific practices and relate it to their scientific identities. This gives students the opportunity to explicitly evaluate the state of their scientific identity.

Here's an example prompt:

Choose two scientific practices that you engaged in within the past unit.

____ Asking questions

____ Developing and using models

____ Planning and carrying out investigations

____ Analyzing and interpreting data

____ Using mathematical and computational thinking

____ Writing explanations

____ Engaging in arguments with evidence

____ Obtaining, evaluating, and communicating information

What activities did you do that supported the scientific practices?

_____

_____

How does engaging in the scientific practices support your identity as someone who can "do science"?

_____

_____

Tip 3 | Ensure diverse representation

Include diverse representations of what scientists look like, where they work, and what they do in both your curriculum and classroom decorations (see Start of the Year p. 34 for decorations resources). In your curriculum, be mindful of the videos you use, of where you are conducting your investigations, and of the perspectives that are included throughout each unit.

One possible activity you could do contains the following steps:

1 Have students draw what a scientist looks like and what scientists do.
2 After completing this individually, they then combine their drawings in groups and present them as a class. This is a great opportunity to discuss the scientific practices and stereotypes of who can do science and where science is done (e.g., by white old men in a lab).
3 Next, have students read from Harvard's "I Am a Scientist" materials and reflect on their misconceptions of what everyday scientists are actually like. This is a great opportunity to humanize scientists as complex individuals and for students to see diverse representations of current scientists in the field.
4 Consider having students redraw their scientists towards the end of the school to see if their conceptions of scientists have changed.

Great Resources
I Am a Scientist, https://www.iamascientist.info

Tip 4 | Teach with asset-based frameworks

Sometimes students are viewed with a deficit lens and this harms students' engagement and impacts the views they have of themselves as science doers. Adopting or strengthening an asset-based framework toward all students means viewing all students as capable and worthy of producing knowledge in your class. This will manifest itself in the feedback that you provide students acknowledging their strengths, in your planning of authentic scientific experiences with the science and engineering practices, and in the high expectations you will hold of the students as doers of science.

> One of my favorite moments in teaching was when I had a student who regularly appeared to be disengaged and had been labeled as a "problem" and not worthy of taking part in our planned lab. This student performed the best on the lab compared to all the other students and shared their love and interest with others through social media. It goes to show that all students deserve the opportunity to engage in authentic science experiences and that the experiences help students see themselves as science doers.
>
> **–HIGH SCHOOL BIOLOGY TEACHER**

Tip 5 | Push back against negativity

There will be moments when fellow colleagues will express deficit comments about students. There will be moments where you might have to decide what coursework a student has to take the next year, or what level they will be in. There will be moments when you are planning and have to choose activities for students to engage in and be exposed to. These are all times when you have the power to push back on negative narratives and frameworks that harm students by actively choosing to support students in the growth of their scientific identities. Whether that is rebutting a colleague with a reframed asset-based comment, recommending detracking in your school, or planning an inclusive and authentic unit, you have the power in your own classroom and own actions to support students' positive scientific identities.

Great Resources

"Detracking in K–12 Classrooms," by Debbie Truong, https://bit.ly/3NoGavX];
Alternatives to tracking, https://bit.ly/3XC1XoZ.

COMMUNITY

Access and Equity

In some school contexts, students are tracked into particular course levels based on labels (e.g., IEP or ESOL) or previous educational grades (failing or "disruptive" students get placed into the lower-track courses). Oftentimes the higher-tracked courses have a disproportionate representation of white students. Students are aware of these dynamics and the messages that they send about their ability to do science. It is especially important as a teacher to combat the negative narratives that students of all tracks carry, such as "I am better at science than those other kids," or "I can't do science, I'm in the dumb class." You might be able to push back against tracking due to disproportionate racial or gender representation or find other ways to advocate for students. Regardless, be aware of these dynamics in school contexts and act in ways to support all of your students' identities.

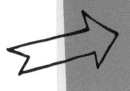

How Do I Establish Two-Way Communication With Caregivers?

Our students' caregivers play an important role in their lives, so consistent communication with those caregivers is one of the best ways to support students. Before reaching out to caregivers, it is important to prepare for your communication and decide how and what you will communicate.

HOW DO I PREPARE TO COMMUNICATE WITH CAREGIVERS?

As an educator, you have a responsibility to

- engage with caregivers from a positive, asset-based mindset,
- use the caregivers' preferred communication mode(s),
- practice what you will say and how you will say it,
- have resources readily available for caregivers to support their learners.

HOW CAN I HAVE A PRODUCTIVE CONVERSATION?

Tip 1   Establish a positive relationship with caregivers

- As a teacher, applying a positive, asset-based mindset to the caregivers of our students is vital to establishing a productive relationship with them.
- In schools, caregivers may be informally characterized as "uninvolved" or "too involved." Whether your desire is for more frequent or less frequent communication, it is important to combat negative views of caregivers, beginning within your own framework.
- Here are some reasons why it is important to cultivate an asset-based mindset when communicating with caregivers:
  - Partnering with caregivers is important to student success.
  - Caregivers have valuable knowledge that can be used to support your students' success.
  - Caregivers are experts on their students and collaboration with them helps students.

Tip 2   Consider the culture of the student

- Norms around communication are deeply cultural. Therefore, it will help if you are aware of the cultures of your students and their caregivers.
- Reflect on the questions that follow to inform your pattern of communication.
  - What do you define as good communication?
  - What are your expectations around frequency of contact and promptness of response?
  - How do you communicate disagreements or frustrations?
- Next, reflect on the following questions that might shed light on differences based on the cultural background of your students and their caregivers. Ask caregivers:
  - What languages are spoken in your home?

- What do you see as my role as the teacher in your student's education?
- How can we collaborate with one another?
- What are some ways you would like to be involved? What could I or the school do to help you be more involved?
- What would you like us to know about your child? What are your child's interests?
- What is working well for your child at school? What isn't?
- What are some ways you would like me and the school to recognize and teach about your child's culture?
- Are there any ways that you feel your culture could be better respected at the school?

- Understanding where your expectations differ from others and learning how to navigate these differences rather than judging them is an important part of having an asset-based approach to caregivers. Make sure to listen no matter what you think of the caregiver. Ask questions and then have caregivers suggest solutions to problems. This prevents them from spending time defending themselves.
- Ultimately, being open to learning about your students and their caregivers and being flexible as you engage in ongoing communication is necessary for successful interaction.

Tip 3 Gather information on how to contact caregivers

- One way to prepare caregivers for contact is by sending a preferences survey home with students for caregivers to respond to.
- This can be sent both electronically and on paper (such as a signed syllabus).
- This survey asks caregivers what their preferred method of communication is (email, phone, text, in person, etc.), their availability, and what their contact information is.
- This is important for caregivers to complete since school communication portals are not always up to date with the caregivers' contact information.
- Before sharing this survey, learn from your students what languages their caregivers speak so that you can work with your world language or counseling department to send home surveys that caregivers can read and respond to on their own. This sends the message that you consider their needs and will do what you can to communicate directly with them.

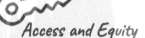

Access and Equity

It is unfair to assume the gender of students and the pronouns they use with their caregivers. Use gender-neutral pronouns, such as they/them/their, until you are aware of the student's preference for pronouns and how the caregivers refer to their student. You don't want to accidentally "out" a student, so double-check with the student on what pronouns to use and with whom.

Consider adding your pronouns to your email signature as a way to clearly communicate your pronouns and as a model for others. To learn more you can visit https://bit.ly/3NkgCRT.

COMMUNITY

Teaching in Flexible Settings

If you have more than 150 students, you may want to send out a letter to all caregivers at the beginning of the year to save time. You can then call, text, or email throughout the year using the caregivers' preferred communication mode.

Sample survey
This survey can be adapted to email or print.

The best way to reach you

Hi, my name is [name], my pronouns are [he/her/they/ze] and I teach [course]. Please complete this survey so that I know how you'd prefer me to reach you this year. I will reach out to share successes with you about your student as well as to ask for your assistance to better support them.

How may I address you? What might I call you in written and verbal communication? Also, please feel free to share your pronouns. _____

1 **What is the best way to contact you?**
  Mark only one choice.
  ___ **Email**
  ___ **Phone**
  ___ **Text message**
  ___ **Written notes home**
  ___ **Other: _____**

2 **Please share your availability. When is the best time for me to reach you?**
  ___ **I can be reached in the early morning 7am–9am.**
  ___ **I can be reached in the late morning 10am–12pm.**
  ___ **I can be reached early afternoon 1pm–3pm.**
  ___ **I can be reached in the late afternoon 3pm–5pm.**
  ___ **I can be reached in the evening 6pm–8pm.**
  Below I will gather information for your contact card. This ensures that student contacts are up to date.

3 **Please share a number where you can be reached. _____**
  _____

4 **Please share an email you check regularly. _____**
  _____

5 **Please share an address where we can send written communication.**
  _____
  _____
  _____
  _____

Access and Equity

It is possible that there are unhoused and/or transient caregivers in your school community. Take care in the way you phrase your questions in the survey. For example, instead of "What is your phone number?" try "What is a number where you can be reached?"

Tip 4 Prepare for the contact

- When preparing for a contact, it is useful to prepare a script or set of notes ahead of time of what you would like to discuss.
- If you are nervous, practicing with a colleague might help.
- Additionally, if you are frustrated, take some time to cool off and revise your responses before making contact with caregivers.
- Keep in mind that you must apply an asset-based approach in all communications with caregivers, even when you are disappointed in or upset with their student or with the caregivers.

Tip 5 Have resources prepared ahead of time

- This will save you time during or after contacting home.
- Common resources might include

- methods for caregivers to access their student's grades (learning management systems, gradebooks, etc.),
- methods for caregivers to access their student's work electronically (Google Classroom, learning management systems, etc.),
- ways students can improve their grade,
- a list of other points of contact the caregiver might want (guidance counselors, etc).

Tip 6 Document the conversation

- Record the content of the communication.
- After receiving a response, record any feedback, such as information shared by caregivers and how you will use it.
- Return to your notes once you've tried a suggestion to record how it worked.
- Plan for your next communication.

Tip 7 Consider the content of the communication

- Ask for perspective and support regarding the student.
- Share important logistical information (field trips, upcoming labs, school events, how to sign on to a learning platform, etc.).
- Share observations of academic behaviors or social/emotional behaviors, including
  - positive behaviors,
  - concerning behaviors; communicate later with an update, hopefully one of positive progress.

Tip 8 Evaluate the impact of the communication

- No communication is perfect, and there is always a chance that something you say can hurt or anger a caregiver.
- If you receive feedback that your words have landed in an unintended way, take note of this feedback for future communication with caregivers and apologize.

WHEN MIGHT I MAKE MY FIRST COMMUNICATION WITH CAREGIVERS?

It is a good idea to have the first communication with caregivers take place within the first two weeks of school. Things that you could include are personal and professional information about yourself (e.g., name, university education, pets, favorite books or science phenomena), all possible methods of communication and boundaries of communication (e.g., times of day, response time of 24 hours), and unique components of your class (e.g., students will have an opportunity to write a science novella). In the first conversations with caregivers, it is helpful to ask how you might best support their student(s) and if there are any questions or concerns they have.

Contacting caregivers proactively and positively about their students helps build relationships early on that help mitigate academic and behavioral issues you might need to communicate about later in the year.

Access and Equity

If you teach in a context with multilingual students and households, finding out what languages are spoken by caregivers, translating communication preference surveys, and gaining access to interpreter services will help you successfully build relationships with caregivers.

If you don't have access to a world language department or accessible translation services in your school, you may use Google Translate to create your survey in different languages to share with caregivers. Use skip logic in Google Forms to ensure caregivers see the questions in their native language.

COMMUNITY

HOW DO I STRUCTURE, ORGANIZE, AND MANAGE MY SCIENCE CLASS?

What you do at the start of the year sets the stage for student-centered learning. It is important to plan for the type of atmosphere you want to create in your classroom. Creating a classroom culture where students feel welcomed and cared for is an important step in building relationships with students. Part of building relationships is asking your students what support they need to successfully engage in learning. Providing time for students to share their needs will help you determine the routines you want to implement. Routines are a set of procedures that, when reinforced and practiced, manage the processes and behaviors of your classroom.

Building familiar routines help students know what to do, why they are doing it, and how they should be working. Creating a predictable learning environment brings a sense of safety for students, and they are more likely to share their thinking with others and reason with the ideas of others in ways that support their engagement in three-dimensional learning.

Routines are also shaped by how you organize and manage your curriculum. If you think about your curriculum's learning goals as well as the trajectory those goals take over the course of a year, the routines and curriculum will be more aligned. Part of that is thinking about how you will support your students in three-dimensional learning. In this type of learning students engage in Science and Engineering Practices (SEPs) to figure out a Disciplinary Core Idea (DCI) as seen through the lens of a specific Crosscutting Concept (CCC). Supporting three-dimensional learning requires you to know how to develop a unit plan and sequence lessons within that plan in support of the learning trajectory.

This chapter answers questions about how to structure, organize, and manage your science class, including the following:

- ☐ **What do I do at the start of the year?**
- ☐ **What are helpful items to stock a science classroom?**
- ☐ **What is three-dimensional learning and how do I engage students in three-dimensional learning?**
- ☐ **How do I get students to engage in the Science and Engineering Practices?**
- ☐ **How can I make science class more student centered and culturally relevant?**
- ☐ **How do I plan a unit?**
- ☐ **What makes a good lesson plan?**
- ☐ **How do I use routines in my classes?**
- ☐ **What norms could I have in my classroom?**
- ☐ **How can I group students?**
- ☐ **What is the role of practice and homework?**

As you read about these topics, we encourage you to reflect on the following questions:

- ☐ **What does this mean to me?**
- ☐ **What else do I need to know about this?**
- ☐ **What will I do next?**

What Do I Do at the Start of the Year?

The start of the school year is a very important time to set the stage for what learning will be like in your class. It will take planning to figure out what you will focus on, how you will decorate and arrange your classroom, and what you will do the first day to set the tone for your students.

HOW CAN I PREPARE BEFORE THE FIRST DAY OF CLASS?

Before the first day of class—even before you see the students—is a great time to reflect on what is important to you as a professional. There are many aspects to consider, such as:

- *Personal intentions.* What do you want to be at the center of your teaching experience? You might say work–life balance, building relationships with students, designing authentic assessments, learning how to co-teach, learning about your building's context, etc. After reflecting, write your intentions down in a notebook. Then reflect on your intentions regularly to see if they are aligning with your practice or talk with a colleague about your intentions.
- *Curriculum/pacing.* Are you familiar with the standards for your classes? Is there a pacing guide accessible to you? What curriculum do you want to use as a resource? Is there a curriculum you can modify, or will you need to make one? After considering these questions, talk with a mentor teacher or your colleagues about any existing resources they would be willing to share. You can also find lots of great resources online through organizations and social media pages that are relevant to your content area (see Learn and Grow p. 154).
- *Materials.* Do you have basic materials for your science class? Some items to consider include markers, colored pencils, sticky notes, whiteboards, dry-erase markers, bins, pencil sharpeners, tape, glue, notebooks, rulers, paper, pencils, and other materials that are specific to your science content for labs that you might teach (see Helpful Items p. 40). Discuss with colleagues what materials exist for you to use and whether or not there is funding available to you to buy more.
- *Collaboration.* Do you have other teachers that you will be co-teaching with? Do you have other content teachers that are teaching the same subjects as you? Start a conversation with your colleagues about sharing resources, pacing, and advice. If you are co-teaching, be sure to discuss the expectations and roles each of you has.

Great Resources

- "5 Tips for Co-Teaching," by Hannah Gross, https://bit.ly/3JsWJWz
- "8 Things Successful Co-Teachers Do," by Ashley Blackley, https://bit.ly/42X12R1
- Questions to ask your co-teacher, https://bit.ly/42Uq6rx
- *Critical Conversations in Co-Teaching: A Problem-Solving Approach* by Carrie Chapman and Cate Hart Hyatt

HOW CAN I DECORATE THE CLASSROOM?

You want your decorations to communicate a welcoming environment and be diverse with respect to the content they are communicating (content, routines, representation, careers, etc.).

Tip 1 | Diverse representation

You want your posters to represent the variety of ways scientists can look, act, and engage in science, particularly with respect to context (lab versus field, solo versus collaborative), race, ethnicity, ability, and gender.

Tip 2 | Celebrating students

If you have existing student work, hang exemplars of each stage of the learning process, such as initial models, common misconceptions, sentence starters with student explanations, and questions. If you don't have existing exemplars, leave space for students to share their work here later.

Tip 3 | Procedures

Display your top five rules/procedures that you want students to follow daily and at all times (see Routines p. 64).

Tip 4 | Content posters

It can be helpful for students to see examples of the content you will be teaching. Additionally, having posters that refer to the Next Generation Science Standards Disciplinary Core Ideas, Science and Engineering Practices, and Crosscutting Concepts can be helpful.

Access and Equity

Posting images that reflect a wide range of people doing and contributing to science can help students see the ways their cultures have supported science and could result in increasing their interest in careers in science.

MANAGEMENT

Great resources:

- Women in STEM, https://bit.ly/3qQt4QA
- Women in STEM, https://bit.ly/44gXbir
- Women in STEM, https://bit.ly/3CJlDxf
- Latinas in tech, https://bit.ly/3NoGQkZ
- NGSS classroom posters, https://bit.ly/3PA1Zvc
- DIY posters on Canva, https://www.canva.com/
- Free resources listed at the National Science Teachers Association, https://www.nsta.org/free

Sources that require a fee:

- Justseeds, https://justseeds.org/
- Teachers should find and get to know local artists in their area to buy posters and decorations from.

Decorations can be costly. If you are allowed to, using fundraising platforms such as DonorsChoose or GoFundMe can be helpful.

HOW CAN I ARRANGE THE FURNITURE IN MY ROOM?

You want to make sure that your room layout is optimized for teacher and student mobility and learning (see Figures 2.1, 2.2, and 2.3.).

Figure 2.1 U-Shaped layout

The advantages of a U-shaped layout are that students are all facing the board for direct instruction and are also able to see one another for whole-class discussions to take place.

Figure 2.2 Mixed-Purpose layout

In this image some desks are in a group and others are facing the board. This is beneficial if you do station work where students either rotate or you are differentiating instruction. Students who are getting direct instruction would sit at the desks facing the board, and students completing an independent group-work activity would sit at the group-work tables. These activities can be occurring simultaneously.

Figure 2.3 Rows layout

Row seating is beneficial for direct instruction as students' attention is focused forward towards the instructor. You might notice the concurrent lab stations. Some science classrooms have lab stations that provide a great opportunity for students to physically transition into group work at these stations.

Tip 1 | Flow

Consider the flow of traffic as students are walking into your room. For example, place notebook bins for students at the farthest point across the room so that students do not get stopped up at the door and thereby block admission for other students.

Tip 2 | Access

Be sure that students have access to the things they need to both see and hear. It is important that students be able to see the front whiteboard or projector from every desk placement in your room. Can all students see the agenda for the day throughout the entire class period? Do you have your trash can(s) and pencil sharpener

Figure 2.4 Daily agenda versus projector

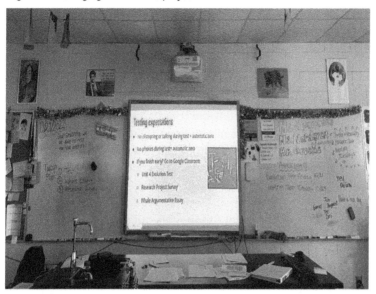

strategically placed where students won't be distracting as they take care of their needs? Do you have a materials station for students to come and get materials for activities (including investigations), or do you have baskets at each table? (Some of these responsibilities can be dedicated to students; see Talk Formats p. 120.)

In Figure 2.4, the daily agenda for the activities, daily learning goals, and important announcements are displayed on the whiteboard so that students can refer back to them throughout the class period. The projector has more immediate directions for what students should be doing at that moment for students to refer to. Having both the whole-class agenda and in-the-moment directions helps students contextualize each learning activity and realize what they should be doing.

As demonstrated in Figure 2.5, if you have multiple classes, displaying announcements, erasing and rewriting daily agendas, and posting announcements and learning goals between classes can be overwhelming. Consider dividing your whiteboard into different sections and have them clearly labeled as such for each class to refer to.

Figure 2.5 Multiple classes agendas

Tip 3 | *Seating charts*

Using seating charts can be an easy tool to learn names and track attendance.

Tip 4 | *Flexible arrangements*

If your class does primarily group work, having the desks in group formation might make more sense for you. Have a flexible room arrangement, if possible, to match the activities with the seating. This might mean rearranging your seating throughout the year multiple times. This is important because it helps with student expectations around an activity and ensures each student has access to the activity. This is more feasible if you ask the students to help you move the desks and limit it to a few times a semester, although you might find it helpful to rearrange multiple times in a unit or a semester (see Figure 2.6). Ultimately, trying this out and observing student responses to the changes can help inform your future actions in rearranging your room.

Figure 2.6 Sample room arrangements by activity

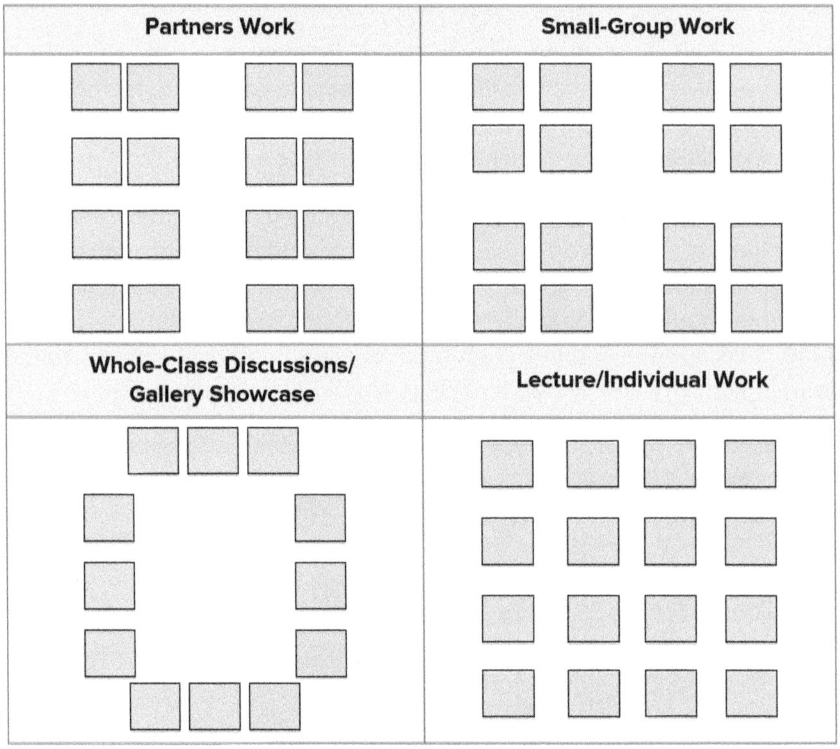

WHAT HAPPENS IN MY FIRST CLASS?

The first day with students is the only opportunity we have to make a first impression with them. It's important to reflect on what message you want to portray about the course (its structures and expectations) and who you are as a teacher. Then plan for the appropriate actions you will take and the activities students will complete the first day that align with your goals. Consider the following:

● How do I welcome students? Starting off with a warm welcome before the class starts can be impactful. This includes greeting students at the door as they come in and helping them find their assigned seats (if you chose to make assignments). Also consider playing music as students arrive.

My favorite first-day activity is to have students build the tallest tower as a group using dry spaghetti and marshmallows. It gives me the opportunity to see how the students problem-solve and interact with one another.

–HIGH SCHOOL BIOLOGY TEACHER

● How do I take attendance? While taking attendance to get to know students the first day, I prefer to call students by last name and have them tell me what they would like to be called from the get-go to help affirm their preferred names and pronunciations. Visual tools to help memorize names could include students making themselves name tents or creating a seating chart.

● What are topics that I might cover? How do you balance communicating important information and setting the tone for the type of class you will be creating? Lecturing the entire day the first day of class would give the impression of a lecture-heavy course. Strike a balance between communicating expectations, setting the tone for your course, and observing the students. Some activities you might use to do this include:

   ● *Alphabetical seating problem-solving.* Students need to seat themselves alphabetically. You can discuss what aspects of this activity are like what scientists do.

   ● *"Get to know you" stations.* Students in groups talk and answer questions at each station (Figure 2.7). Each station's questions align with the goal of that first week of getting to know students academically and personally (e.g.,what are their favorite restaurants).

Access and Equity

It is important to use gender-neutral language when first addressing students until you get to know their pronouns. Consider asking students privately their pronouns through a Google Form or other survey, or having students make name tents for their desk to help you both memorize names and visually see pronouns. You can model pronoun use when you introduce yourself.

MANAGEMENT

Figure 2.7 Students' favorite places to eat

What Are Helpful Items to Stock a Science Classroom?

Necessary supplies for a science classroom will typically include materials that support lab activities. In addition, some supplies will support activities that are helpful for group work, literary research, and communications. Some supplies can be acquired as you need them; some are helpful to have in place before the school year begins.

WHAT ARE HELPFUL ITEMS FOR *EVERY* SCIENCE CLASSROOM?

Your needs for equipment will be informed by the discipline of science you are teaching; a crucial list for teaching biology will be different from a list for physics. This kind of distinction is most often applicable to high school teachers, but there are items that every science teacher uses, regardless of specialization. These items allow students in any course to measure distance, time, mass, force, volume, and temperature, and they provide the infrastructure for basic experiments or explorations.

Measuring Devices	Lab Use	Consumables	Instruction
• Meter sticks • 12-inch or 30-cm rulers • Stopwatches • Balance (triple beam) or electronic scale • Spring scales (pull type) • Graduated cylinders • Thermometers (NSTA recommends alcohol or electronic)	• Safety goggles • Eye droppers • Ring stands • Clamp-on rings for ring stand • Gas (best) or alcohol heaters/burners • Rubber bands • Flashlight or other point source of light • Tongs • Tweezers • Magnifying glasses	• Duct tape • Masking tape • Clear (Scotch) tape • Paper towels • String (white cotton works well) • Water balloons • Cardboard • Highlighters • Glue sticks • Gloves • Soap	• Whiteboards for each student • Dry-erase markers • Calculators, depending upon student need • Scissors for each group

WHAT ARE HELPFUL ITEMS FOR SAFETY AND FOR EACH SCIENCE DISCIPLINE?

In chemistry, lab instructions typically begin with lists of the equipment and chemicals that you will need to prepare for the lab. Some items are universally needed. Note that the first list contains safety equipment recommended to always be on hand when chemicals are handled.

In physics, you will need some tools that support motion, some for optics, some for electricity and magnetism, and some for waves. In biology, you will see many experiments that call for the same equipment as is listed under chemistry.

Safety Equipment (needed for all classes in which chemicals are present)	Chemistry Equipment	Physics Equipment	Biology Equipment
• Enclosed goggles that seal around the eyes • Gloves rated to accommodate handling chemicals • Eye-washing station, or bottles of eye wash and cups to treat a spill to the eyes • Hand-washing station with soap and running water • Apron or lab coat • Proper way to dispose of chemicals • Towels for drying hands and wiping down benches	• Glass beakers • Plastic beakers • Test tubes • Erlenmeyer flasks • Eye-drop dishes • Molecule (stick and ball) sets • pH paper or electronic pH meter • Heat source (Bunsen burner or hot plate) • Tongs • Crucibles • Funnels	• 1-kg weight (best if it has a hook on it) • Collision carts • Motion detectors • Concave and convex lenses • Plane mirrors • Long slinkies • Light bulbs • Wires with alligator clips • Strong magnets, flat if possible • Resistors • Rheostats • Voltmeters • Prisms • Mirrors • Pendulums • Spring balance • Batteries	• Microscopes (both binocular and monocular) • Petri dishes • Test tubes and test tube racks • Microscope slides and cover slips • Heat source (hot plate or burners) • Beakers • Erlenmeyer flasks • Funnels • Graduated cylinders • Droppers • Pipettes

A note about ordering equipment: A typical equipment order assumes that students work in groups, often of four. For that reason, many teachers will order eight items, each item going to a single group. If you have thirty-two students in a class, there will be eight groups of students with four students in each group.

WHAT ARE HELPFUL INSTRUCTIONAL ITEMS TO HAVE IN PLACE?

Here are some documents that science teachers use:

- a syllabus for the year—make sure you employ any templates that your school or district might require,
- a safety contract signed by students and parents (see Great Resources sidebar for examples),
- state standards for your course (likely virtual),
- if you use rubrics, then a rubric template.

Great Resources

"How to Write a Syllabus," by Jennifer Gonzalez (https://www. cultofpedagogy.com/ course-syllabus -how-to/); rubrics and templates (bit.ly/3Ydqv6U); examples of safety contracts (https://bit. ly/3ZPoNtq or https:// bit.ly/409ZCla).

What Is Three-Dimensional Learning and How Do I Engage Students in Three-Dimensional Learning?

Three-dimensional learning involves more than students learning science content. It involves students doing science to learn science ideas and being able to connect those ideas to ones that are common to all science disciplines. This is a switch from the way science has traditionally been taught, but it provides students with a science education that will help them to understand the world in a new way. First, we'll discuss what makes up three-dimensional learning and teaching, and then we'll provide ways to engage students in doing three-dimensional learning.

WHAT IS THREE-DIMENSIONAL LEARNING AND TEACHING?

Three-dimensional learning and teaching as articulated by the Next Generation Science Standards (NGSS) is a process in which teachers focus on three aspects of science:

- Disciplinary Core Ideas,
- Science and Engineering Practices,
- Crosscutting Concepts.

Without intentional focus on these three aspects, students (and teachers) may concentrate more on the facts of science and less on *doing* science. With a three-dimensional approach, students do the fun and engaging work of figuring out and making sense of phenomena. In this way, students are motivated to learn since they are trying to answer a specific question in the real world.

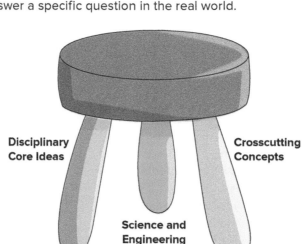

Source: iStock.com/Ogieurvil

WHAT ARE THE DISCIPLINARY CORE IDEAS?

The Disciplinary Core Ideas (DCIs) are the main ideas in science that top scientists and educational researchers have determined through extensive study are important for a person to understand in their K–12 science career. These ideas organize the discipline and help us to understand and investigate complex

Great Resources

A Framework for Science Education by the National Research Council offers a vision of how students can learn science effectively. This document, which can be found at https://bit.ly/3NMhhvW, provided the basis for the Next Generation Science Standards.

The Next Generation Science Standards at https://www.nextgenscience.org/ provide standards for this vision.

relationships in science. A deep understanding of these ideas and an ability to apply them helps students to see science in the world around them and provides a coherent understanding of how the world works. The DCIs are learnable at different depths as students go through their K–12 science careers.

The four main subject classifications within the DCIs are

- Physical Science (PS),
- Life Science (LS),
- Earth and Space Sciences (ESS),
- Engineering, Technology, and Applications of Science (ETS).

Each of these ideas is broken down into two to four numbered subheadings.

Access and Equity

Relating the DCIs to the interests and life experiences of students is important since the authors of the NGSS have this as one of the criteria of what to include in the classroom. You can help by relating the DCIs to aspects of your students' lives (see Unit Planning p. 56; Culturally Relevant p. 52).

MANAGEMENT

Physical Sciences	Life Science
PS1: Matter and Its Interactions	LS1: From Molecules and Organisms: Structures and Processes
PS2: Motion and Stability: Forces and Interactions	LS2: Ecosystems: Interactions, Energy, and Dynamics
PS3: Energy	LS3: Heredity: Inheritance and Variation of Traits
PS4: Waves and Their Applications in Technologies for Information Transfer	LS4: Biological Evolution: Unity and Diversity
Earth and Space Sciences:	**Engineering, Technology, and Applications of Science**
ESS1: Earth's Place in the Universe	ETS1: Engineering Design
ESS2: Earth's Systems	ETS2: Links Among Engineering Technology, Science and Society
ESS3: Earth and Human Activity	

Each of those numbered subheadings is broken down again into more subheadings, and the subheadings are further broken into elements that describe what students are figuring out about that idea. Figure 2.8 shows how the DCIs are broken down and provides an example of one element of one Life Science subheading. Pay attention to these elements as these are the ideas that anchor lessons.

Figure 2.8 Example of how the DCI on biological diversity is broken down into smaller ideas

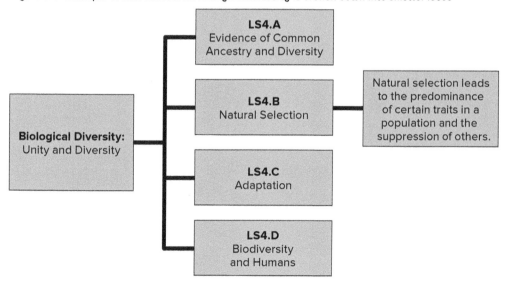

WHAT ARE THE SCIENCE AND ENGINEERING PRACTICES?

Great Resources

This book is an excellent resource for teachers who want to help students see the connections between the important science concepts so they can understand our natural world and solve problems:

Disciplinary Core Ideas: Reshaping Teaching and Learning, edited by Ravit Golan Duncan, Joseph Krajcik, and Ann E. Rivet, https://bit.ly/3Xodc3T

The SEPs reflect what professional scientists and engineers do in their work. When students participate in these practices in science class, they are involved in figuring out answers to questions that they have about our natural world. They gain an understanding of the nature of science and engineering instead of just reading about it. Both science and engineering use similar practices, but scientists primarily ask questions and engineers primarily define problems. In science, the goal is to construct explanations for phenomena, whereas the goal of engineering is to design solutions using science ideas. (For more on this, see Practices p. 48.)

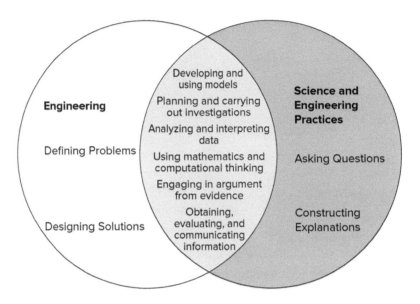

The intent of three-dimensional learning is that engineering be integrated into the teaching of science. As students define problems, they can use engineering to design solutions based on the DCIs that they have learned.

WHAT ARE THE CROSSCUTTING CONCEPTS?

The Crosscutting Concepts (CCCs) are big ideas that are evident across science. These concepts help students understand the world and connect knowledge across disciplines and grade bands. The concepts provide coherence for students and give them a lens through which to see the world. When teaching a DCI, it is best to focus on two or three CCCs so that students are not overwhelmed. For example, when studying systems, students might look at the CCC of energy and matter. To bring more CCCs into what students are trying to figure out could be complicated and confusing.

The CCCs include

- Patterns,
- Cause and Effect: Mechanism and Explanation,
- Scale, Proportion, and Quantity,
- Systems and System Models,
- Energy and Matter: Flows, Cycles, and Conservation,

- Structure and Function,
- Stability and Change.

There is a tendency in science teaching to look at the DCIs as separate from each other, but focusing on a CCC helps students to see the connections across courses and in the real world. For example, a student in biology can better understand cellular respiration and photosynthesis by connecting them to energy transfer and energy transformation from a previous physics class.

HOW DO THE THREE DIMENSIONS WORK TOGETHER?

The three dimensions are combined to form a performance expectation, which articulates what students should be able to do and understand by the end of your instruction. Performance expectations are used for assessment.

Let's put it all together:

1 Students engage in the Science and Engineering Practices
2 to figure out a Disciplinary Core Idea
3 as seen through the lens of a specific Crosscutting Concept.

Great Resources

An in-depth description with examples of each CCC can be found in *Crosscutting Concepts: Strengthening Science and Engineering Learning*, edited by Jeffrey Nordine and Okhee Lee, https://bit.ly/3NKgPOU.

MANAGEMENT

Performance Expectation		
Students who demonstrate understanding can:		
MS-LS2–4 Construct an argument supported by empirical evidence that changes to physical or biological components of an ecosystem affect populations.		
Science and Engineering Practices **Engaging in Argument From Evidence** • Construct an oral and written argument supported by empirical evidence and scientific reasoning to support or refute an explanation or a model for a phenomenon or solution to a problem.	**Disciplinary Core Ideas:** **LS2.C: Ecosystem Dynamics, Functioning, and Resilience** • Ecosystems are dynamic in nature; their characteristics can vary over time. Disruptions to any physical or biological component of an ecosystem can lead to shifts in all its populations.	**Crosscutting Concepts:** **Stability and Change** • Small changes in one part of a system might cause large changes in another part.

Each of the three dimensions has a progression across the grade bands where new and existing knowledge is linked to previous ideas. The ideas are revisited and connections built on so that students see the big picture (instead of unconnected facts) of science.

Thinking about the three dimensions in science education has totally changed how I teach science and how students learn. I've seen a huge change in student engagement by including practices and with students being able to connect their ideas when using the Crosscutting Concepts.

—MIDDLE SCHOOL SCIENCE TEACHER

What Is Three-Dimensional Learning and How Do I Engage Students in Three-Dimensional Learning?

45

HOW DO I ENGAGE STUDENTS IN THREE-DIMENSIONAL LEARNING?

All of the three dimensions work together to help students participate in science education that relates to their life and helps to explain natural phenomena.

Here are some tips to get you started.

Tip 1 One way to make science learning three-dimensional is to first pick out at least one element of the Disciplinary Core Ideas

Tip 2 Choose a phenomenon that leads students to figure out this core idea

Tip 3 Choose at least one Science and Engineering Practice that students will do that relates to the core idea and the phenomenon

Tip 4 Select one or more Crosscutting Concepts that connect with the core idea and practice

You can see in the example task that follows that students take part in both science and engineering. (For more on this, see Unit Planning p. 56; Practices p. 48; Lesson Planning p. 60.)

Steps in Constructing a Three-Dimensional Lesson	Example
Element of a Disciplinary Core Idea	For any pair of interacting objects, the force exerted by the first object on the second object is equal in strength to the force that the second object exerts on the first, but in the opposite direction.
Phenomenon	A sled crash into a tree (illustrated by video)
Science and Engineering Practices	Students could ask questions and then plan and carry out investigations about the impact of collisions between a small sled and different objects. After students analyze and interpret their data, they figure out that for every action there is an equal and opposite reaction. Then they could design a way to minimize the damage done in a collision.
Crosscutting Concepts	Students see that there is a cause-and-effect relationship between the size of the sled and the impact of the collisions. This could help them predict what would happen in natural or designed systems.

Here's another example: The learning could focus on the CCCs of energy and matter. Energy is a concept that connects the ideas of how energy transforms from chemical to kinetic energy in food chains to produce water (Life Science), the cycling of water through Earth's systems driven by energy from the sun and the force of gravity (Earth and Physical Sciences), and how we might use energy to desalinate water to drink (Engineering). This type of thinking helps students to understand how energy shows up in the different DCIs. See Figure 2.9 for a way to illustrate this idea.

Figure 2.9 How energy and matter interact in the world

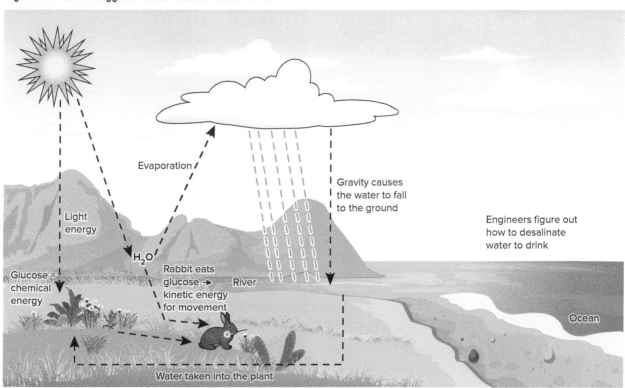

Light energy

Evaporation

H₂O

Glucose = chemical energy

Rabbit eats glucose → kinetic energy for movement

River

Water taken into the plant

Gravity causes the water to fall to the ground

Engineers figure out how to desalinate water to drink

Ocean

MANAGEMENT

HOW CAN I THINK ABOUT THREE-DIMENSIONAL LEARNING?

Think of a science fact or idea as a single brick: Many students in the past have ended up with a pile of bricks when they graduate. They know many things about science, but these things are not connected or usable. If we encourage students to learn the DCIs while doing the SEPs, they can use science facts and the practice of building to create a brick house. When we tie in the CCCs, student knowledge is held together much like bricks are held together with mortar. Which is more useful, a pile of bricks or a brick house?

Source: pile of bricks from istock.com/owattaphotos; brick house photo by Karen Mesmer

How Do I Get Students to Engage in Science and Engineering Practices?

Great Resources

Resources on teaching about a solar eclipse, https://go.nasa.gov/42TPpKC/

Students use the eight SEPs to help them see how knowledge develops in science, how to make sense of the world around them (for science), and how to design solutions to problems (for engineering).

The practices include

- asking questions and defining problems,
- developing and using models,
- planning and carrying out investigations,
- analyzing and interpreting data,
- using mathematics and computational thinking,
- constructing explanations (for science) and designing solutions (for engineering),
- engaging in argument from evidence,
- obtaining, evaluating, and communicating information.

A key to having students engage in SEPs is to choose a phenomenon that will be a good fit for teaching the DCIs that students are to learn. (For more on the DCIs, see Three-Dimensional Learning p. 42.) A natural phenomenon is an event that is observable and occurs in nature. Students investigate and use their science knowledge to explain the phenomenon.

For example, you could show students a video of a solar eclipse to help them figure out how a model of the solar system can explain eclipses of the sun.

 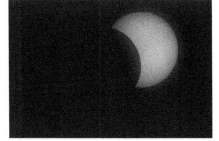

Source: Photos by Robert Rolley

For a better idea of how students might engage in the practices when explaining the solar phenomenon, this table pairs scenarios of student engagement and the practices.

Practice	Student Engagement in the Practice(s) to Explain the Phenomenon
Asking questions	Students share what they notice and wonder about the solar eclipse. The class could choose the question about how solar eclipses happen so that they have a class-identified question.
Plan and carry out an investigation	Students can choose classroom objects to use, but you may want to have on hand flashlights for the sun, an inflatable globe for the Earth, and a golf ball for the moon to see if students decide to use these for their investigation.

Practice	Student Engagement in the Practice(s) to Explain the Phenomenon
Develop and use a model Constructing explanations Engaging in argument from evidence Obtaining, evaluating, and communicating information	• As students plan and carry out their investigation, they can also **develop a model** about how a solar eclipse happens. • To **create possible explanations** of the solar eclipse, two groups could work together to **argue from evidence** as a way to build consensus. • This larger group could then **communicate their model to the class**, and in turn the class can **argue** to decide which model best **explains** the eclipse. The class could even put parts of different **models** together to create an explanation. • This consensus model could then be extended to answer the question about why the eclipse is seen first in the west and then in the east.
Analyze and interpret the data	A teacher could also bring in data about when solar eclipses occur and have students analyze and interpret the data to help them predict the next eclipse.
Using mathematics and computational thinking	Students could use mathematics and computational thinking in analyzing the data of graphs of the moon's lines of nodes to help them predict the next eclipse. They also could look at a calendar of the predictions of solar and lunar eclipses to see if they can find a pattern.

Great Resources

OpenSciEd has a middle school lesson that is similar to this example: Unit 8.4 Earth in Space, Lesson 7, https://bit.ly/42ZPrAu. They have many other lessons as part of storylines that incorporate SEPs.

All-science curricula, https://www.openscied.org/

MANAGEMENT

In this scenario, students do not just come up with an answer to questions and the teacher isn't the arbiter of right or wrong. Students are making sense of phenomena and engaging in a process of questioning, figuring out, and refining as they share their ideas with peers. They are actively doing and thinking, not just by themselves but with a scientific community in the classroom. (For more on building a science community, see Community p. 10.) Teaching science with SEPs helps students to build conceptual understanding as well as make connections to the world around them.

When I was a student in science class, I listened to the teacher, took notes, and answered multiple-choice and true/false questions on tests. I got most of the questions right, but I didn't know how science worked and didn't really have a clue how science ideas came to be. I see now that science students need to participate in the process of science by actually engaging in the science practices.

–MIDDLE SCHOOL SCIENCE TEACHER

How Do I Get Students to Engage in Science and Engineering Practices?

49

WHAT IS A SCIENTIFIC MODEL AND HOW DO STUDENTS USE THEM TO CONSTRUCT EXPLANATIONS?

Scientific models are constructions to show how something works in our universe. Models can take the form of a drawing, a three-dimensional object, words, equations, or computer simulations. They are related to explanations since models explain and predict. But they are more than just representations. A ball-and-stick representation of carbon dioxide is not a true scientific model. But if it is used with a similar representation of water (H_2O) to show how a chemical reaction takes place and carbonic acid is formed, then it could be considered a model. In other words, just showing what something looks like is not explaining, but using manipulatives to show how chemical reactions take place is one way to explain how a process occurs.

The SEPs are integrated and often intersect. Scientists and engineers argue about their models and about their explanations. As data is analyzed and interpreted, scientists often start to begin constructing a model by identifying the parts of the model and the relationship of those parts and how they interact over time. This could lead to new questions and planning out new investigations.

As a scientific practice, constructing models and explanations involves finding the relationships between variables and also how or why phenomena happen. Students are asked to back their claim with evidence and also add reasoning that ties together the claim and evidence with science principles.

HOW DO THE WAYS THAT STUDENTS DO SCIENTIFIC AND ENGINEERING PRACTICES PROGRESS OVER TIME?

Students will need to use the SEPs many times over in their careers as science students. The complexity and sophistication of a practice increases as students progress through the grades. In early elementary, students are expected merely to indicate what a model is, but by high school, they are deciding which model meets their explanatory needs.

Here is an example of a few of the elements associated with the progress of the SEPs over time.

K–2 Practices	3–5 Practices	6–8 Practices	9–12 Practices
Distinguish between a model and the actual object, process, and/or events the model represents. Compare models to identify common features and differences.	Identify limitations of models.	Evaluate limitations of a model for a proposed object or tool.	Evaluate merits and limitations of two different models of the same proposed tool, process, mechanism, or system in order to select or revise a model that best fits the evidence or design criteria. Design a test of a model to ascertain its reliability.

Source: Appendix F: *Science and Engineering Practices in the NGSS*, p. 6 https://bit.ly/3YULtaX

HOW DO THE DIFFERENT PRACTICES INTERSECT?

The practices do not work separately from each other. They also do not emerge in a particular order during instruction. As Figure 2.10 shows, students ask questions while they are doing any of the practices. They argue about their explanations, designs, and models. They use mathematics and computational thinking when analyzing and interpreting data about the investigations that they have planned and carried out.

Figure 2.10 How the science and engineering practices are used

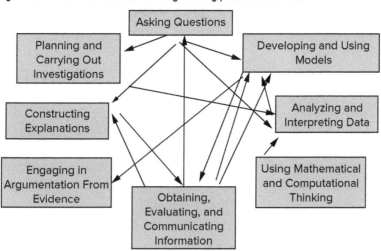

Great Resources

To read more about why we teach SEPs instead of the scientific method, go to https://bit.ly/3PlQwQ2.

MANAGEMENT

In other words, students will be using many SEPs in the course of a lesson.

Great Resources

These two resources give more information about how to have students ask questions:

- Wonder and Notice Protocol, https://bit.ly/4443w04
- The Question Formulation Technique, https://bit.ly/3jjkwyn

An in-depth description with examples of each SEP can be found in *Helping Students Make Sense of the World Using Next Generation Science and Engineering Practices*, edited by Christina V. Schwarz, Cynthia Passmore, and Brian J. Reiser, https://bit.ly/3WrUcjV.

How Can I Make Science Class More Student Centered and Culturally Relevant?

Students learn best when they are

- empowered to learn,
- central to the learning process through active participation,
- learning content relevant to their lives.

HOW DO I LEARN ABOUT MY STUDENTS' INTERESTS AND CULTURES?

The first thing to do to make your science class more student centered and culturally relevant is to get to know your students (their cultures, interests, etc.). While there are a variety of ways that this can happen, it is important that you treat this as a continual learning process and that you hold space to get to know your students throughout your entire time with them (see Identities p. 21).

HOW DO I INCORPORATE WHAT I LEARN ABOUT STUDENT INTERESTS AND CULTURES INTO MY SCIENCE TEACHING?

After getting to know your students, the next things to do are to unit plan and lesson plan with their interests in mind, have multiple and diverse representations, and select relevant phenomena.

Tip 1 Choose phenomena that align with students' interests, identities, and/or local context

When first introducing a unit or lesson, anchoring it with phenomena is an important beginning step (see Lesson Planning p. 60). There are many resources devoted to helping you find phenomena, and there are helpful factors to consider when lesson planning. To support cultural relevance, consider these three factors:

1 students interests,
2 their identities,
3 their local context.

These factors relating to students' lives will engage and affirm students' identities in your class.

Tip 2 Make a Driving/Discussion Question Board

One of the NGSS scientific practices is to ask questions. In beginning a unit, making a driving question board together as a class can be an affirming way to have all of the students' perspectives and voices heard (see Figure 2.11).

Figure 2.11 Water unit driving question board.

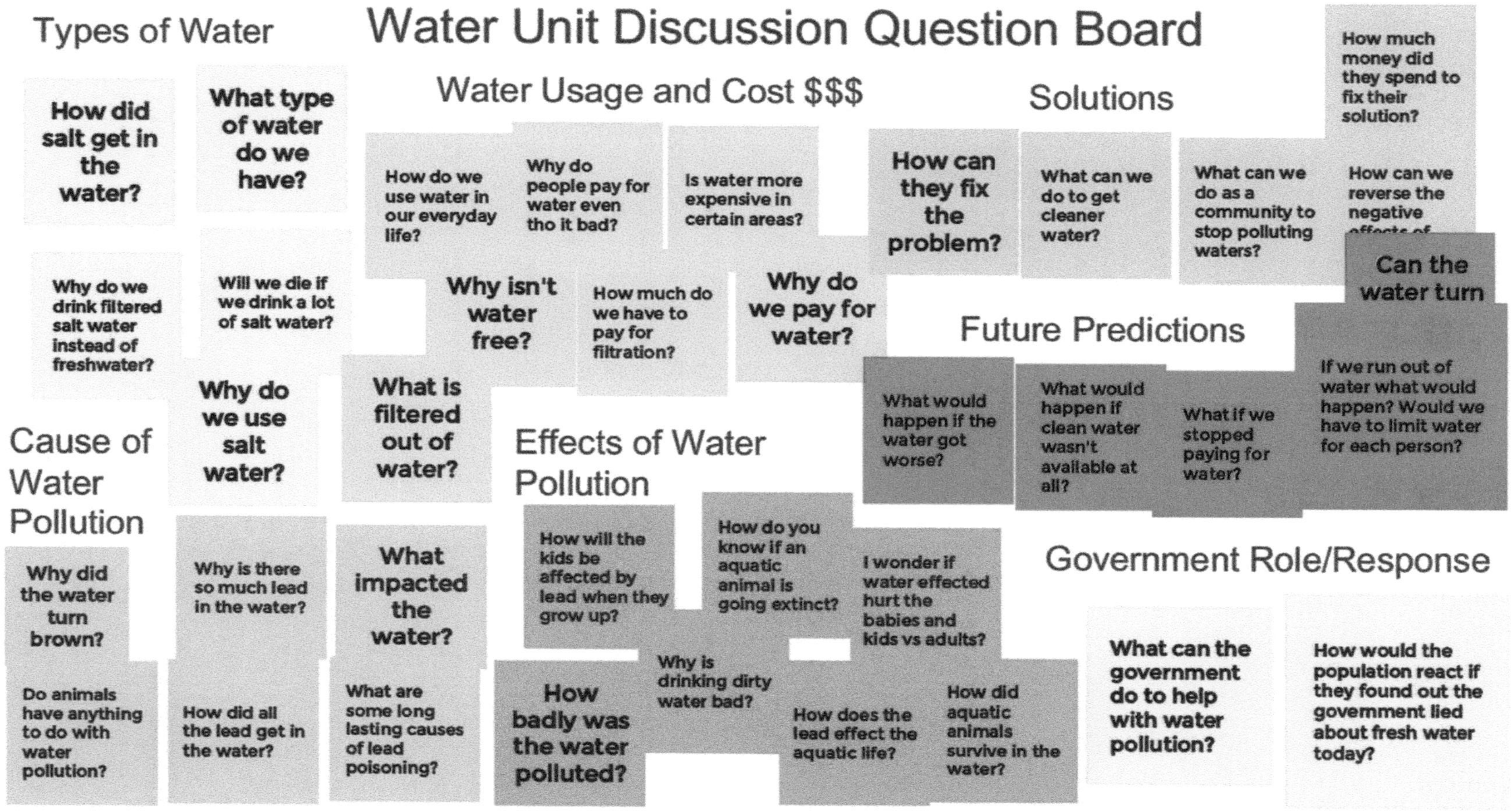

Water Unit Discussion Question Board

Types of Water

What type of water do we have?

How did salt get in the water?

Will we die if we drink a lot of salt water?

Why do we drink filtered salt water instead of freshwater?

Why do we use salt water?

Cause of Water Pollution

Why is there so much lead in the water?

How did all the lead get in the water?

Why did the water turn brown?

Do animals have anything to do with water pollution?

Water Usage and Cost $$$

How do we use water in our everyday life?

Why do people pay for water even tho it bad?

Is water more expensive in certain areas?

How much do we have to pay for filtration?

Why isn't water free?

What is filtered out of water?

Why do we pay for water?

Solutions

How can they fix the problem?

What can we do to get cleaner water?

What can we do as a community to stop polluting waters?

How much money did they spend to fix their solution?

How can we reverse the negative effects of

Can the water turn

Future Predictions

What would happen if the water got worse?

What would happen if clean water wasn't available at all?

If we run out of water what would happen? Would we have to limit water for each person?

What if we stopped paying for water?

Effects of Water Pollution

What impacted the water?

What are some long lasting causes of lead poisoning?

How will the kids be affected by lead when they grow up?

How do you know if an aquatic animal is going extinct?

Why is drinking dirty water bad?

How badly was the water polluted?

I wonder if water effected hurt the babies and kids vs adults?

How does the lead effect the aquatic life?

How did aquatic animals survive in the water?

Government Role/Response

What can the government do to help with water pollution?

How would the population react if they found out the government lied about fresh water today?

Students start with noticings and wonderings from the student-centered/culturally relevant phenomena you choose, then write and share their favorite questions with the class. Students group similar questions together (see Routines p. 64).

(see Routines p. 64)

Tip 3 · Design units and lessons with students' questions in mind

Predicting student questions for any given phenomena can help you plan your units and lessons (see Unit Planning p. 56; Lesson Planning p. 60), but you will not be able to predict them all, especially when students represent different cultures and experiences. Including activities in your unit/lesson to learn student questions and elicit student answers to their own questions is an important aspect of affirming students' perspectives and making your lessons more culturally relevant.

Tip 4 · Incorporate a variety of assessments

Having a variety of assessments for students to express their learning and making sure those assessments are authentic to the phenomena and problem you are trying to solve is another strategy for making your instruction more student centered. This might mean, for example, involving the students' broader community as an intellectual resource, or using rubrics for projects rather than a multiple-choice assessment (see Assess Learning p. 132).

HOW DO I EMPOWER STUDENTS THROUGH STUDENT CHOICE AND VOICE?

Students are more invested in the learning process when they have the opportunity to choose what it looks like. Consider giving students a choice in both their assignments and groups. This could be letting students choose from a variety of representations for their final project, choose their favorite way to learn a new concept, form their own groups, or choose the roles that they want to play during group work.

Here are some examples of how students might exercise agency with the NGSS Science and Engineering Practices.

Science and Engineering Practices	Student Choices
Asking questions	Students choose what questions they want to ask and focus on.
Developing and using models	How do they want to represent their models? Students might lean more heavily on written descriptions, drawings, or the presentation aspects of their model. How do students want to use their model or another's model? Let students choose what feedback to provide or how to incorporate revisions to their models.
Planning and carrying out investigations	Students can choose or create their own steps for procedures or their own question that they want to explore in their investigation.
Analyzing and interpreting data	Students might interpret data differently with all their different experiences and perspectives. Students can choose how to represent their own data and discuss these representations with other groups for evaluation.

Access and Equity

Co-teachers are specially trained in modifying and increasing access and opportunities for students when it comes to assessments and lessons. Co-developing your classroom activities and/or providing co-teachers with sample work before lesson implementation can support you in learning ways to develop more inclusive resources for student learning and assessment.

Using mathematics and computational thinking	Oftentimes there are a variety of ways students can solve or use mathematics for any one given problem, so let students choose which way makes the most sense to them. Let them choose the questions/problems they want to answer with this type of thinking.
Constructing explanations	Give students choice in what their claims are, which pieces of evidence are relevant to them, and which perspectives they want to address in their explanation.
Engaging in arguments from evidence	Students can choose which arguments they want to compare, the evidence that they address, the ethical implications, the critiques that they give/receive, how they represent their argument (written, orally, etc.), and the relevant factors (societal, economic, ethical, environmental, etc.).
Obtaining, evaluating, and communicating information	Have students choose which information they want to evaluate from which sources. Lastly, there are a variety of ways that students can communicate information (written, verbally, visually, etc.). Let students choose how to represent and communicate their information.

HOW DO I CONTINUE TO LEARN ABOUT CULTURALLY RELEVANT TEACHING?

It is important that you continue to grow in your own cultural identity and cultural competence. This could be attained by reading relevant resources, being in conversation with colleagues that represent diverse backgrounds, joining organizations, following educational social media accounts, and so on.

Here are some suggestions to help you continue to grow in your journey to more culturally relevant teaching.

Books	
Culturally Relevant Teaching and the Brain by Zaretta Hammond	*Science in the City* by Bryan A. Brown
Culturally Sustaining Pedagogies: Teaching and Learning for Justice in a Changing World, edited by Django Paris and H. Samy Alim	*The New Teacher Book: Finding Purpose, Balance, and Hope During Your First Years in the Classroom* by Linda Christensen, Stan Karp, Bob Peterson, and Moé Yonamine
	Organizations
	National Association of Multicultural Education (NAME)
Websites	**Articles**
7 Culturally Responsive Teaching Strategies and Instructional Practices, https://www.hmhco.com/blog/culturally-responsive-teaching-strategies-instruction-practices Culturally Sustaining Pedagogy, https://ready.web.unc.edu/section-2-transforming-practice/module-17/	"Culturally Relevant and Culturally Responsive: Two Theories of Practice for Science Teaching," by Felicia Moore Mensah, https://bit.ly/3DGgyGG

Great Resources

There are a variety of teaching techniques that allow student voice and choice to come through so that students are generally speaking and analyzing more than the teacher. Some of these include Socratic Seminar, Jigsaw, Concept Mapping, Chalk Talks, Fishbowl, Concept Attainment, and Four Corners. You can find descriptions of these techniques at https://bit.ly/44Nb4Wt.

MANAGEMENT

How Do I Plan a Unit?

Have you ever read a mystery novel where the clues are laid out bit by bit and then you figure out toward the end "whodunit?" This type of story keeps you engrossed because you are trying to make sense of what is happening. You know the question that you are trying to answer and are putting together the clues to figure out the answer. A science unit that reflects this type of process is called a storyline. Using storylines enables the teacher and the students to know where they are going with the learning and what problem they are trying to solve. Problem-based learning (PBL) projects are another format for teaching a unit and are discussed in PBL Overview p. 86 and PBL Process p. 90.

A storyline includes

1. one or more of the DCIs,
2. a phenomenon,
3. a driving question,
4. connected lessons that build understanding of the DCIs to explain the anchoring phenomenon. The SEPs and at least one CCC are interwoven in each lesson.

WHAT IS A PHENOMENON?

A storyline starts with a *phenomenon,* an observable natural event. This helps students to anchor their learning in a real-world situation, just like a mystery novel starts with a specific crime that is trying to be solved. Examples of phenomena include a terrarium that has been closed for many years, a sled stopping when it hits an object, or a solar eclipse. In traditional science instruction, a unit focuses on teaching a topic, such as evolution, that students may or may not apply to new situations. In this scenario, students learn facts about evolution through lectures on how evolution happens.

A phenomenon-based approach gives students a reason to investigate and a reason for learning. For example, students can investigate why tortoises native to the same group of islands have different carapace shapes. Knowing the mystery they are to solve helps them figure out the problem at hand.

Great Resources

- To find out more about using phenomenon in lessons and units, visit https://bit.ly/3XkIyIW.

These resources will provide more information about using phenomena and provide ideas for phenomena that you can use for units and lessons:

- Using Phenomena in NGSS-Designed Lessons and Units, https://stemteachingtools.org/brief/42

- Qualities of a Good Anchor Phenomenon for a Coherent Sequence of Science Lessons, https://stemteachingtools.org/brief/28

- The Wonder of Science: Phenomenon, https://thewonderofscience.com/phenomenal

HOW DO I DESIGN A STORYLINE?

Here's an example of a storyline.

Action	Example
Step 1: Choose a DCI or a few related ideas.	Natural selection leads to the predominance of certain traits in a population and the suppression of others. (MS-LS4–4)
Step 2: Find a related anchoring phenomenon that leads students to understand the science ideas you identified.	Some Galapagos Island tortoises have dome-shaped carapaces, while others have a saddle-shaped carapace.
  *Source:* Photos by Karen Mesmer	
Step 3: Introduce a phenomenon to the students and ask them for their ideas about how to *explain the phenomenon.* Do not tell them why the phenomenon exists—they need to figure this out.	In the case of the tortoises, some students might say . . . • The saddlebacks needed to reach food, so they stretched their necks. • Two different species of tortoises bred and made tortoises with a different-shaped carapace. • The two types of tortoises have always been like that since they have existed on Earth. (These ideas are not supported by scientific evidence, and it is important during the storyline to provide evidence to students that indicate these explanations did not happen.)
Step 4: Construct a driving question.	• Students can help write the question after experiencing the phenomenon. • It could be very specific, such as "Why do Galapagos tortoises have different carapaces?" or more general, such as "How do we get different species on Earth?" Driving questions help focus student learning.
Step 5: *Craft a series of lessons* that support students in reasoning and sense-making about the phenomenon.	Each lesson starts with a phenomenon plus a question, with students doing science practices and relating what they find out back to the Galapagos tortoises.

Access and Equity

Storylines are guided by student questions, and students should see that they are making progress in explaining the phenomenon. This benefits students with a wide range of achievement since they are helping to choose the direction of the storyline. There may be deviations from the intended sequence of lessons to address some of the questions and interests of students. When applying the explanation or model that students constructed from the original phenomenon, different or new phenomena to explain can be given to students to speak to their current understanding.

Great Resources

- "Designing Coherent Storylines Aligned with NGSS for the K–12 Classroom" by Brian Reiser, https://bit.ly/3GObKBx

- To read more about storylines, go to https://www.nextgenstorylines.org/. There are full-length storyline units for elementary, middle, and high school at this site.

- To read about how a teacher developed a storyline, see "A Recipe for Planning an NGSS Storyline: Curiosity, Persistence, Reflection and a Library of Resources," by Wanda Bryant, https://bit.ly/3Nqb5lv.

In our tortoise example, you may want to start with the idea that there is *variation in a population*. A question could be, "How are Asian beetles different from each other?" A related phenomenon would be a sample of beetles, presented as specimens (dead or in photos) that have variations. Students can investigate the variation in this population and relate variation in beetles to variation in tortoises. This would be a first step in developing a model of natural selection and an explanation of how living things change over time. Lessons would then follow on *selective advantage* as well as *survival, reproduction, and heredity*, leading to *how populations change*. The initial natural selection model that students started developing with the concepts of population and variation can be added to or revised with the new evidence provided in these additional lessons. There may be various models to explain natural selection and adaptation so students can argue with others in the class about those models and explanations to come up with a class consensus model. They can then apply this model to a new phenomenon that it can also explain, such as bacterial resistance. They can extend their explanation to artificial selection (MS-LS4–5) by working on a case study about, say, racing sled dogs in the Iditarod in Alaska: "How do you breed dogs to be a part of a team and run fast?" See this approach mapped out in Figure 2.12.

Figure 2.12 Possible storyline for the driving question "How do we get different species on earth?"

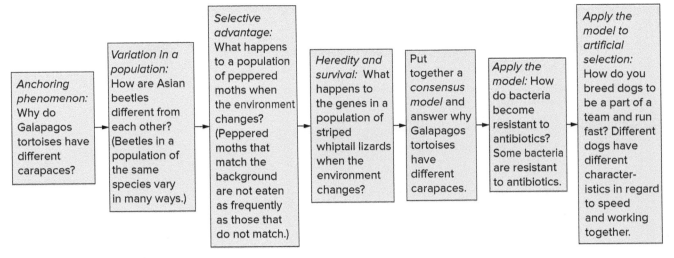

Answers to Your Biggest Questions About Teaching Secondary Science

In using storylines, the students are doing the work of putting together the pieces of the puzzle to come up with a consensus explanation and/or model to answer the driving question and explain the phenomenon. They are part of a scientific community in the classroom.

> *Teaching is like telling a story. You have the beginning where you launch your lesson. In the middle, students can participate in investigations, readings, and discussions. Finally, you have the end, where we reach our goal and answer the driving question. If I was to tell them the "why" to start, we wouldn't get to the higher and deeper level of thinking (and all the other fun activities I have planned along the way)!*

—SEVENTH-GRADE TEACHER

WHY USE STORYLINES?

Using storylines to create units switches the teacher's role from being the person who gives the answer and asks students to confirm it to one who guides the students to figure out the answer for themselves. Mystery novels do not tell you "whodunit" at the beginning then give you the clues that they used to find the answer. They also don't provide a multiple-choice test at the end to see if you memorized all the clues and the answer. In the same way, science education that mimics the approach of mystery novels by providing a coherent way for students to learn and understand the DCIs as well as the SEPs and CCCs is engaging and gives students a reason to care about the material. When students participate in the process of making sense of phenomena, they do the work of science, just like professional scientists.

Great Resources

Some examples of storylines that are free Open Educational Resources include:

- Grades 1–12 (Quality Examples of Science Lessons and Units), https://bit.ly/3WFghel
- IHub Chemistry, https://bit.ly/3Wu9ILZ
- PEER Physics, https://bit.ly/3PVMPyC
- Illinois science teacher storylines (biology), https://bit.ly/3Jyt7oN

What Makes a Good Lesson Plan?

Planning is an important part of teaching science. You want to make sure that in-class activities help students learn science ideas as well as engage them in the SEPs. An important part of learning science ideas is to help students make connections across different disciplines in science. A lesson plan template that includes learning science ideas, engaging in the SEPs, and making connections across science disciplines through the CCCs can be helpful when planning a lesson.

HOW DO I PLAN MY LESSONS?

Planning the outline of a unit in a storyline format helps students learn science in a way where one lesson leads to the next to help explain a phenomenon (see Unit Planning p. 56). It is a good idea to have unit storylining precede planning a single lesson since each lesson leads to the next one, and up-front planning will help you make connections between and among lessons. Start with an outline of the entire unit and then plan all the details of each lesson from there. The driving question is the same for the whole unit, with a related question for each lesson. An anchoring phenomenon extends through the entire unit, and there is a lesson-level phenomenon for each lesson.

Here's an example of a lesson plan template.

Date:	
Driving question of the unit:	
Lesson question to be answered:	
Description of the activity:	
What is the learning target of the lesson? (Shared with students. It can be written as an "I can . . . " statement)	
What phenomenon will be used? How will students share their observations and questions about the phenomenon?	How will students use the Disciplinary Core Ideas to explain the phenomenon? Provide a link to the standard that this addresses.
What Science and Engineering Practice(s) will students use to make sense of this phenomenon? How do they use them?	What Crosscutting Concept(s) will be used and how?
How will students share their ideas?	How will you ensure equitable participation with students?
What is the flow of the lesson? 1. 2. 3. 4.	How will you assess students?

WHAT ARE THE PARTS OF A LESSON-PLANNING TEMPLATE?

Let's break down the parts of the lesson-planning template:

1. Each unit in a storyline format has a *driving question* that guides the learning. A possible driving question for a storyline involving heredity could be, "Why do we look something like our parents, but not exactly?" Each lesson would answer part of the question, with an answer tying all the lessons together at the end.

2. Each lesson starts with a *lesson-level question*. This question is related to what you want students to figure out in the lesson. A lesson question related to the driving question above could be, "How are parents and their offspring alike and different?" Then you can *describe the activity* that students will do, such as matching pictures of offspring with their biological parents and describing similarities and differences between the generations.

3. The *learning target* is shared with students so that they can see what they are going to be asked to make sense of in the lesson. It is often in the form of an "I can . . . " statement so that students are able to evaluate whether they have met the targeted learning for the lesson. Ideally, the statement does not "give away" the answer to the lesson question, but it could mention a science practice to explain what students will be doing. A CCC such as cause and effect can also be included. For example: "I can plan and conduct an investigation to explain the effect of the size of a magnetic force at different distances."

4. A *phenomenon* is an event that occurs in the universe that can be explained with science. An anchoring phenomenon for a unit is important for students to be able to connect their ideas to the real world. They see that they are figuring out a problem instead of just learning about a science fact. They are able to see connections between what they are learning in science class and in the world outside of that class. (See Unit Planning p. 56; Culturally Relevant p. 52.)

    Having a different phenomenon for each lesson helps focus student learning and build their understanding of how to figure out the answer to the driving question. Have students share questions that they have about the phenomenon and identify a class question that will be answered during the lesson.

Great Resources

Here are some resources that will provide ideas for phenomena that you can use for units and lessons:

- Phenomena for NGSS, https://www.ngssphenomena.com/
- Social-justice phenomena for the classroom, https://www.ngssmacroscope.com/
- Phenomena Finder, https://bit.ly/3XkPl58

(For more information on the next three parts, see Three-Dimensional Learning p. 42.)

(For more information on the next three parts, see Three-Dimensional Learning p. 42.)

5   How do students use the *Disciplinary Core Idea(s)* to explain the phenomenon?
    The DCIs are important science concepts. In this section, you will describe how these science concepts explain the particular phenomenon that you chose.

6   What *Science and Engineering Practice(s)* do students use to make sense of this phenomenon? How do they use them? Here is where you will describe what SEPs students use and what they do with those practices to figure out an explanation for the phenomenon (see Practices p. 48).

7   What *Crosscutting Concept(s)* are used? How are they used?
    What particular lens do students use when looking at the phenomenon? These are the CCCs. They may focus on systems and system models, or energy and matter, or any one of the other five CCCs.

8   How will students share their ideas? (See Discourse p. 114.)
    Students need many opportunities to *share and argue their ideas* based on evidence. They can share them verbally and also in text. Other ways for students to share include gestures such as a thumbs-up or a thumbs-down, symbols, or graphs.
    During each lesson, you could provide students with time to think first. Then they share their ideas with partners, then with groups, and finally with the whole class. This is done so that students share questions about the phenomenon, what they notice, and possible explanations.

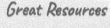

Great Resources

Prompts to help teachers probe student understanding of crosscutting context as they investigate phenomena, https://bit.ly/46glcZ1

Great Resources

The A/B Partner Talk Protocol at https://bit.ly/3Nq5i5P helps students know how to talk when they are reasoning about science ideas. This type of protocol provides a scaffold for students to collaborate and reflect on how their partner's ideas have influenced how they think.

- The Talk Activities Flowchart at https://bit.ly/3prusZz helps you plan for student talk in your classroom. It consists of a flowchart that helps you figure out different talk activities to try.

- Inclusive and Equitable Discussions, https://stanford.io/3XJZ84r

- Physics resources, https://bit.ly/45LTKSK

Access and Equity

One way to help students know how to start sharing their ideas is with sentence starters. These give students who may not know what to say, especially multilingual learners and students gaining comfort with academic language, a more structured way to be heard.

9   How will you ensure equitable participation with students? (See Discourse p. 114; Talk Formats p. 120.)
    You want to make sure that all students have a chance to share and participate. Calling on eager hand raisers, students who seem to know the answer, or compliant students does not ensure equitable participation (see the Great Resources sidebar above).

10 What is the flow of the lesson?
    This is a brief outline of how you see the lesson progress through the class time. For example:

    a   Bell ringer (which could be the phenomenon)
    b   Activity #1
    c   Activity #2
    d   Assessment

> As a new science teacher, it is easy to get caught up in teaching the "facts" of science. Following this lesson-planning structure forces you to move away from older methods of teaching science, which focused on "fact collecting" by students, and move to phenomena-based science education. Students are always providing evidence for scientific principles and answering the important question, "How do we know what we know?"

—FIRST-YEAR SIXTH-GRADE SCIENCE TEACHER

11 How will you assess students? (See Assess Learning p. 132 and Formative and Summative Assessments p. 136 for more information.)
    Decide whether your assessment will be formative, whereby you have students share their understanding during or after a lesson, or summative, in which the assessment comes at the end of a unit or lesson set. Choose a format to assess students and then decide how to proceed with the next lesson based on the feedback from the students.

How Do I Use Routines in My Classes?

Routines help structure the learning environment for students so that they know what is expected of them during class. Some routines can be generalized to any classroom, but this section focuses on routines that are specific to science classes. We also provide recommendations on how to prepare for and implement your classroom routines.

WHAT ARE EXAMPLES OF DIFFERENT ROUTINES?

Routine 1: Driving/discussion question boards. One of the scientific practices that students are asked to engage in is asking questions. One routine to help facilitate this is creating a discussion or driving question board. Oftentimes this is a routine that takes place at the beginning of a unit and is revisited throughout the unit.

- *Students observe a phenomenon.* This can be done in a variety of ways, such as a notice and wonder chart, or through taking notes or observing with their senses (see Sense of Wonder p. 13).
- *Students generate questions about the phenomenon.* This can be done by having students brainstorm questions individually or collectively. The Question Formulation Technique (QFT) encourages students to generate as many questions as possible without judgment. Have students be supportive and nonevaluative of one another's questions. Students can then revise their questions to become more open-ended instead of closed.

Here are some examples of how questions can be transformed from closed ended to open ended.

Closed-Ended Questions	Open-Ended Questions

• Answer options are limited to short explanations or one-word answers (yes, no, etc.).
  • Example: Is the human population on Earth changing?
	• Answer options require long explanations or have more than one correct answer.
	  • Example: How is the human population changing on Earth?

- *Students create the board.* Each student writes down a question of interest to them (usually on a post-it note) and shares it with the class. Students should be respectful in listening to one another's questions. Questions could be grouped thematically and placed on a board that is visible in the room (see Figure 2.13). Each class might come up with different questions, so having space for multiple class ideas is important.

Tip   If you want each class to have their own physical board, using giant post-it notes, reusable post-its called wipeboards, trifolds, or extra unused whiteboard space can be helpful in separating the boards while also keeping them accessible

Figure 2.13 Sample discussion question boards focused on exploring a local phenomenon of climate change: peach production levels in Georgia

WHAT DO I DO WITH THE QUESTIONS WE GENERATE?

As a way to affirm students, you could use the questions to help you plan lessons and units. For example, a student might ask, "Why are some peaches fuzzy?" and this could inspire you to teach a lesson on plant/fruit adaptations. Some questions can even be used as extension lessons in the unit as a way to differentiate for students (see Differentiation p. 107; Lesson Planning p. 60). At the end of lessons, revisit the board to see if there are new questions to be added or if the questions that have been answered help students see learning progress being made.

Routine 2: Investigations. Another important scientific practice for students to engage in is planning and carrying out investigations. Consider the following in your investigation routines:

Teaching in Flexible Settings

Question boards can be made through virtual whiteboard apps such as Jamboard.

- *Safety.* Clearly communicate safety routines that are specific to your investigation context (lab, outside, etc.). This includes modeling and discussing appropriate behaviors (such as walking instead of running, no eating, etc.).
- *Procedure.* Help students clearly understand each step of the procedure whether they planned the procedure or not. Students might need to see a demonstration of a specific technique in the procedure and have the opportunity to practice it with feedback (for example, pipetting into a gel electrophoresis well).
- *Materials.* Tell students where the materials are and provide them with all the materials that they might need. Additionally, communicate to students how they will clean up their materials and plan for them to have enough time to do so.

Routine 3: Modeling. Developing and using models is another important scientific practice for students to master. When using models, consider the following routines:

- *Generating a model.* Models can take diverse forms whether electronic, written, or drawn. Giving students individual time to generate a model first gives them an opportunity to participate in developing a class consensus model later. When communicating expectations to students about generating their first model, emphasize that the model should be clear to others and used as an explanatory tool.
- *Revisions.* Have students hold on to their initial models or have a classroom model as a reference for them to return to and revise. Have students evaluate one another's models in partners or through a gallery walk, or provide feedback on their models directly as the instructor. Clearly communicate expectations for appropriate feedback. What is most important is that students are given the opportunity to revise their models based on feedback and additional data.
- *Materials.* Oftentimes for written or drawn models, students can use whiteboards to share their models with others while also easily revising the models. For electronic models, sharing explicit directions on how to generate their model and navigate the model is helpful for students. See Figure 2.14, Figure 2.15, and Figure 2.16 for example models.

Figure 2.14 Initial and final class consensus models about peach production in Georgia.

Answers to Your Biggest Questions About Teaching Secondary Science

Figure 2.15 Initial and final individual student models about levels of organization in environmental science with student feedback sticky notes aimed at helping to revise the model.

Figure 2.16 Original and final models for the different levels of the environment.

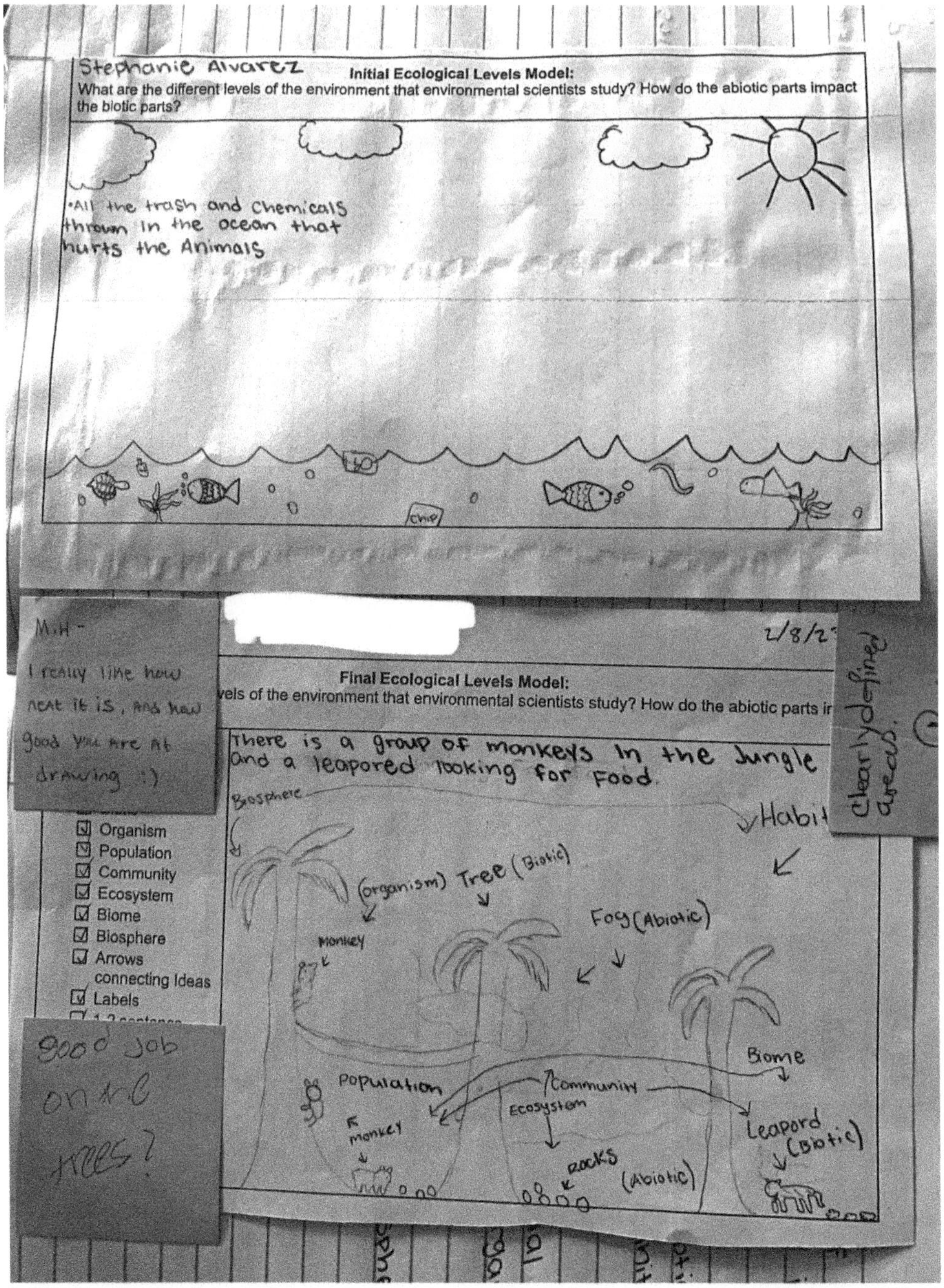

Routine 4: Community culture. It is important to continuously provide a supportive learning environment. Plan every couple of weeks for the class to revisit the classroom culture. This is a time to develop relationships with and among students, revisit classroom norms, and reflect on the state of the classroom community culture (see Community p. 10).

ADDITIONAL ROUTINES TO CONSIDER INCLUDE:

- *Beginning of class.* What do you want your students to be doing at the beginning of class each day?
- *End of class.* How do you want students to end the day? How do you want students to leave your class?

Teaching in Flexible Settings

Models can be made online using a variety of virtual tools, such as PowerPoint, Google Drawings, Jamboard, BioRender, or SageModeler. A student could save these to a folder for reference later.

Answers to Your Biggest Questions About Teaching Secondary Science

- *Group work.* How will groups be structured? Where will they work? What are their roles? (See Grouping p. 74.)
- *Attention signals.* How will you get the students' attention when they are in the midst of an activity?
- *Entering/leaving the class.* How do students leave to use the restroom? What does a student who arrives tardy do? How do you document this?
- *Individual work.* How could students be respectful of others when completing individual work? What could students be doing to ensure their individual success at this time?
- *Materials.* How and where will students get the materials they need (pens, pencils, papers, etc.)? How will they return them?
- *Technology.* What technology is or is not appropriate at this time? How could technology (phones, computers, etc.) be used for this activity?
- *Classroom management.* How will you intervene and redirect students not following expectations? How will you document your attempts?

Consider providing instructions describing your routines for students to refer to. If the instructions are specific to an activity, they could be on the board or on the actual assignment students are doing. If the routine is something more general, such as a beginning-of-class routine or a leaving-the-classroom routine, you might have a written poster or set of instructions in a physical location that makes sense for that routine.

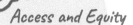

Access and Equity

Emergent multilinguals and students with diverse abilities might benefit from particular routines. If you have a supporting teacher, discuss with them what routines would be best for the students and set expectations for how both of you will model or reteach routines.

MANAGEMENT

> *I love having students complete bell ringers, a mini-activity to be completed at the beginning of class. It is a great opportunity for students to review content from the previous class, access prior knowledge, or engage them in socio-emotional learning.*

–HIGH SCHOOL SCIENCE ESOL TEACHER

HOW DO I IMPLEMENT ROUTINES?

When implementing your routines, here are some important tips to consider.

Tip 1 The beginning of the year is the best time to teach routines

Routines need to be explicitly taught. Students don't automatically know where to go, what to do, or when to do things. Take the first few weeks of school to model appropriate routines and behaviors. Then give feedback on and reteach the routines and behaviors as needed.

Tip 2 Be consistent in implementing these routines and giving students feedback on their demonstration of the routines

Tip 3   Compliment students when they are following procedures correctly

Framing routines and behaviors in positive terms helps students know what is expected of them. Reframing negative behaviors into positive ones helps students focus on what they should be doing instead of not doing. For example, instead of "Do not run," say, "Do walk."

Tip 4   Routines take time to learn and are context specific

Grading students on their behavior or compliance with a routine does not measure their academic performance or understanding of a concept. Instead, explicitly reteach students and provide them with consistent feedback.

Notes

What Norms Could I Have in My Classroom?

A norm is a standard or expectation of behaviors for a group of people. One example would be, saying "Salud" or "Bless you" after someone sneezes. Norms are important because they directly impact how people collaborate and communicate with one another. In the school context, norms in a classroom define how students and the teacher behave toward and respond to one another in their learning community. These norms help support a positive learning community.

You may include any norms that you and the students need in order to create and maintain a positive scientific learning community. Think about establishing these norms at the beginning of the school year so that students can engage with them from the get-go. Sometimes these norms are suggested by your school or department, but identifying norms that will be helpful for your own classroom is important as well. There may be some classes in your building that do not have norms similar to yours, and this may create some issues for students. It is still important to create norms for your class so that students understand what is expected of them when they are with you.

Consider the following when articulating your norms:

- What do you as the teacher need to positively support students in their science learning?
- What do the students need to engage in their scientific community and to learn science?
- What can both you and the students give to one another as a scientific learning community?
- What are three to five general classroom norms that you can reference and that your classroom community needs?
- What are the activity-specific norms that your students will need for things such as investigations, group work, individual work, etc.?
- Where in the room will you display your general classroom norms so that you can go back and reference them regularly?

If you need help gathering ideas for norms, consider an activity at the beginning of the school year in which you pose reflection questions for students to answer. Examples include:

What structures do you need to learn in a classroom?
What did your favorite teacher do to support your learning?
What did your least favorite teacher do to inhibit your learning?
What does respect look like to you?

Publicly discuss the results. Explicitly agreeing on how you, the teacher, will behave and student agreement on the norms can help establish a co-constructed classroom community.

Access and Equity

Norms exist in every context and are often implicit and culturally situated. For example, depending on one's cultural background, it might be an appropriate norm to call instead of texting for communicating. Therefore, it is extremely important to reflect on your own culture and those of your students and their families to make classroom norms explicit and agreed upon.

MANAGEMENT

It is also not a bad idea to give your own norms to the students. Lin and Perry (2022) suggest that giving norms instead of letting the group set them helps to include everyone, particularly those with marginalized identities. The norms they suggest are:

1   Impact is greater than intent, so own your impact and examine, investigate, and interrogate your intent.
2   Ask for what you need and tell what you can give.
3   Ask for what others need and what others can give.

(Used with permission of Learning Forward, www.learningforward.org. All rights reserved.)

Teaching in Flexible Settings

In an in-person setting, students can generate norms or give feedback on norms individually through Google Forms or Pear Deck, or collaboratively on whiteboard platforms such as Jamboard or Nearpod. Students can comment on one another's posts as a way to affirm fellow classmates.

Source: Illustration by Joshuah Thurbee, Knowles Teacher Initiative

HOW DO I MAINTAIN MY CLASSROOM NORMS?

Once your norms have been established, keeping them a relevant part of your classroom practice is important.

Here are some tips to help you support using your norms throughout the school year.

Great Resources

"Should Groups Set Their Own Norms? Maybe Not," by Joyce Lin and Ayanna Perry, https://eric.ed.gov/?id=EJ1333747

Tip 1   Reflect

● Reflect on the norms as a classroom community to see how they are being followed, what impacts they are having, and why they are important. These reflections help remind all participants in the classroom community of their roles and impacts.

Tip 2   Change is okay

● A classroom community is made of living students and teachers who naturally grow and change over time. It is normal and encouraged for the school community to change its norms as community members reflect on them.

Tip 3   Reference visual reminders

● Having a reference point for both you and the students to refer back to the norms serves as a reminder for students as they are engaging in their learning community.
● Norms may be posted in a place where all students can see them and be referenced as needed.

- General norms may be displayed on a wall, such as on a classroom poster.
- Display activity-specific norms on student assignments, on the projector, or on a whiteboard (see the example that follows).

Tip 4 · Model the norms

- Especially at the beginning of the year when the norms are being introduced, it is helpful for students to see an example of a norm being enacted.
- By modeling your expectation or mindset for any given activity, you are supporting your students with an example of what to do.

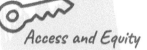

Access and Equity

Co-teachers and paraprofessionals have specific training on behavioral expectations that can help create an environment that is more inclusive and accessible to students (e.g., ESOL, IEP/504). Talking with your supporting teachers and paraprofessionals about what norms are important and how to enact them is a productive conversation to have at the beginning of the school year and throughout the rest of your time together.

Question Formulation	
Directions:	Norms:
In groups, you will determine who will write down the questions and who your team members are. The goal is to come up with AS MANY QUESTIONS AS POSSIBLE! Do not stop to judge or evaluate them! You should have at least ten questions as a group.	• This is group work—everyone should participate and do work! • Accept everyone's ideas (do not judge). • Invite people to share if they have not shared already.

Tip 5 · Encourage accountability consistently

- One of your responsibilities as the teacher is to ensure that students are following the norms. By intervening consistently and compassionately, you can redirect and remind students of the norms for the purpose of supporting the positive classroom environment that students need.
- Students can communicate to you how they would like to be held accountable in ways that are humanizing and supportive of them. For example, some students would prefer to be redirected on the norms privately rather than publicly.
- Hopefully students can help keep one another accountable to these norms too.

MANAGEMENT

How Can I Group Students?

Science is a collaborative activity and the idea of a lone scientist working on their own without sharing with others is a myth. Scientists work in teams to plan and conduct investigations. They develop and use models and construct explanations, and they argue over findings and about other aspects of science. Peer-reviewed journal articles are often written by multiple authors and include acknowledgments of other scientists that the authors have worked with. The accomplishments in science have all been achieved by scientists working together.

To have students do SEPs in a classroom, they need to work together. There are different ways to group students depending on the goals of the lesson or unit and the ways a teacher wants students to interact (see Lesson Planning p. 60; Unit Planning p. 56).

WHAT ARE THE OPTIONS FOR GROUPING STUDENTS?

Identity & Agency

To support students in developing this awareness, share with them diverse groups of scientists who have contributed to the discipline (see Sense of Wonder p. 13).

Get to know your students at the beginning of the year. As you observe their work and how they interact in class, you can identify different characteristics about them that will be useful when dividing them into groups. You can also survey them about their interests, about what attributes they identify in a successful group, and what practices and participation structures they are familiar with and which ones they have difficulties with or need to learn. Establishing norms for working in groups helps all students participate equally (see Norms p. 71).

HOMOGENEOUS GROUPING

You may want to have students who are similar in various ways or who have similar interests work together.

Homogeneous Grouping
Ways to group students:
<ul><li>Group those who are able to combine ideas and have been taught to understand a phenomenon.</li><li>Group those who have similar interests.</li><li>Group those who have the same perseverance and ability to work together at their own pace.</li></ul>
Benefits:
<ul><li>From formative assessment, you can determine the students who are able to combine ideas they have been taught and use those ideas to develop a model, construct an explanation, or solve a problem. You may then want to group these students together. This is especially helpful when applying a model or scientific principle to a novel situation. There could be various case studies for different groups, with some being more complex than others. Those groups who have already had experience with thinking through difficult tasks could work on applications that are more complex. For example, you may find from formative assessment that some students may be able to explain how variation in a population relates to selective advantage, survival, reproduction, and heredity. Other students may not see the connections between these aspects of natural selection yet. Students could be grouped based on their responses to an assessment on the relationship between these ideas.</li><li>Having similar interests can help with group cohesion. This can help with perseverance as students focus on a particular problem.</li><li>Another characteristic that can be used to place students in homogeneous groups is the ability to work together at a similar pace.</li></ul>

Homogeneous Grouping (*Continued*)

Drawbacks:

- There may not be a variety of ideas about ways to approach a problem.
- There might be groups who struggle to put together complex ideas in the time that is allotted.
- Students may assign a higher status to groups who work more quickly or on more complex problems and lower status to groups who do not.
- If students are grouped by a characteristic other than academic achievement, high-performing students may do more of the work and not include everyone in the group.

Ways to alleviate problems:

- If there is not a variety of ideas in a group, the teacher can propose some new ideas as they work with different groups.
- If a group is struggling to put together complex ideas, the teacher can provide some questions to support them.
- Establish norms for treating others and their contributions with respect.
- Include strategies that ensure that all students are sharing their reasoning, equally contributing work, and communicating what they understand. These strategies could include a Discussion Diamond, Claim-Pass, or Idea Coaching, all of which are found in the Talk Activities Flowchart mentioned in the Great Resources sidebar.

HETEROGENEOUS GROUPING

Forming groups that include students with different characteristics can be beneficial in many instances. Here are some ways to heterogeneously group students and the benefits of those groupings.

Heterogeneous Grouping

Ways to group students:

- Group them by reading level, math computation skills, or drawing skills.
- Group them by confidence in planning and conducting investigations.
- Students with different approaches to solving problems could be grouped together.
- Group those with a range of facility with combining complex ideas to understand a phenomenon.
- Give a phenomenon probe that consists of a question with possible answers to reveal the alternative conceptions and initial ideas students have about a core idea. You can group students with different ideas.

Benefits of each type of grouping:

- Looking at *reading skill* may be helpful if you have an assignment that involves gaining information from texts or interpreting texts to make decisions about next steps. Those who have a higher level of reading facility can assist those who may have difficulty. The same is true for *mathematical computation or drawing skills*.
- Grouping those who have a *deeper understanding of planning and conducting investigations* with those who struggle can help each group be successful. This can be true of other practices also, such as developing and using models and constructing explanations and designing solutions.
- When you group students who have *differing ways of thinking*, there may be some students who are linear thinkers and some who are more creative in the way they solve problems. Having both of these types of thinking in a group can provide more diversity so that more types of solutions can be examined.
- Students with differing strengths can support one another's learning. For example, some students are able to easily link complex ideas, others can see links between scientific systems, and others can ask questions that support the development of clear arguments.

Great Resources

Understanding Student Thinking Through Formative Assessment, https://bit.ly/43aJOzL; Uncovering Student Ideas Probes, https://bit.ly/3Juy6sF

(Continued)

Access and Equity

Avoid using heterogeneous grouping to have higher-achieving students help you solve classroom management problems in your classroom. Heterogeneous grouping is beneficial for students who have different ideas so that they can share them. Homogeneous groups help since students have the opportunity to work on materials that are a fit for their strengths and areas where they need work. They each have their place in the science classroom.

Heterogeneous Grouping (*Continued*)
• When you give a *phenomenon probe* that indicates student alternative conceptions, students can be assigned to a group with those who have differing answers. They can then argue their ideas with others based on evidence. Lessons that help them understand why some of the answers are not scientifically accurate could follow their initial discussion.
Drawbacks:
• High-achieving students may do more of the work and not include everyone in the group. • If students have different ways of thinking, some students can continue to think that their idea is better even when provided with evidence to the contrary. • If students have different ways of thinking, other students can be disparaging of ideas that are different from their own.
Ways to alleviate problems:
• Include strategies that ensure all students are sharing the work and that they all understand. These include a Discussion Diamond, Claim-Pass, or Idea Coaching, all of which are found in the Talk Activities Flowchart mentioned in the Great Resources sidebar. • Establish, emphasize, and assess norms to support respectful disagreement. • Emphasize that, in science, empirical evidence is used to back claims.

SELF-SELECTED
Students can select their own groups.

Self-Selected
Ways to group students:
• Students select their own groups within certain parameters. • Students could be grouped based on a certain number per group, grouped with people they haven't worked with before, or grouped with those they know that they can work well with.
Benefits:
• This allows students to have a choice in their learning, and they may become more involved and engaged because of this. • They can be taught to recognize characteristics in their peers that are beneficial to them so they choose students they can work well with.
Drawbacks:
• Sometimes there can be groups who are not productive and become distracting. • Groups often lack diversity in their way of thinking about a problem and do not consider other alternatives. • Some students can feel left out if they are not chosen to be a part of the group.
Ways to alleviate problems:
• Norms can be developed to guide students' selections and to deal with any drawbacks.

RANDOM GROUPING
Students can be assigned randomly to a group.

Random Grouping
Ways to group students:
• Names can be written on popsicle sticks and a prescribed number chosen for each group. • Students can count off by the number of groups needed and then all the students of the same number join together. • An app such as a random number generator can be used to assign students to groups.

Great Resources

The Talk Activities Flowchart at https://bit.ly/3prusZz helps you plan for student talk in your classroom. It consists of a flowchart that helps you figure out different talk activities that can be used in groups.

Random Grouping *(Continued)*
Benefits:
• As long as students see that the groups are formed randomly, they may be more willing to work with everyone who is in their group. • It eliminates students preventing others from joining them in self-selected groups. • Students may work with those who they have never worked with before and gain new perspectives.
Drawbacks:
• Some students may be uncomfortable working with the students in their group.
Ways to alleviate problems:
• Establish norms about how to act in a group. • Be available when problems arise and help them think through ways to solve problems in their group.

Varying the way you group students throughout the year is important. It is beneficial if students have the experience of working with many different classmates to be able to think about differing views. Argumentation skills can be developed more successfully when students think differently, but groups who think similarly may be able to complete tasks more efficiently.

—HIGH SCHOOL BIOLOGY TEACHER

HOW OFTEN COULD GROUPS BE CHANGED?

There may be times when a teacher wants a quick share with pairs and then sharing with a group of four during a class discussion. This ensures equal participation from students. Those groups may only last for part of a class session. Other times teachers may want to change groups for each lesson. A benefit of changing groups is that this provides for a variety of different ideas in each group. In addition, students will need to learn strategies for working with other students. This would mimic what they experience in the world outside of science class. Drawbacks of changing groups include losing the cohesion of keeping a group together for a unit.

What Is the Role of Practice and Homework?

The issue of homework has been a somewhat controversial topic in the past 20 years, but recent research has yielded a now commonly held understanding: Homework for middle and high school students is correlated with higher achievement. We recommend assigning homework, but it must be done deliberately, with careful attention to the hoped-for student learning. Consider having almost every homework assignment accompanied by feedback.

Great Resources

"Does Homework Improve Academic Achievement? A Synthesis of Research," by Harris Cooper, Jorgianne Civey Robinson, and Erika A. Patall, https://bit.ly/3JowEHZ

WHY IS ASSIGNING HOMEWORK USEFUL?

Homework allows for greater student time and effort in the subject area, and at a more detailed level. It can help to:

- Provide practice in skills taught in class. Skill-practicing homework is common in classes heavier in math, such as chemistry and physics.
- Prepare students for classwork. If you are to have a class discussion in a Socratic Seminar, students must have read something first and be prepared to discuss it.
- Provide an outlet for student creativity. Students who write stories, make videos, or create their own problems often find themselves more engaged in the work.
- Reinforce ideas in the longer term as they study for assessments or prepare for class.
- Move students toward greater personal agency and independent learning.
- Provide a platform for feedback.
- Offer the teacher more opportunities for formative assessment.
- Provide the students with opportunities to engage in work outside the classroom, such as projects where students engage in the community.

Note that there can be overlap among the rationales listed above. A student can build up their agency while practicing the balancing of chemical equations, for example.

Teaching in Flexible Settings

If students have access to tech provided by the districts or local libraries, this opens the range of the types of assignments that can be given. If students do not have access to tech outside of school, you might refrain from assigning homework that requires such access or allow students to use their school-based devices to do any tech-dependent homework problems during class time.

Identity and Agency

It is important that students have some choice in how much practice they are required to do for homework. One strategy for student agency is to provide an assignment with a large number of problems available for practice but to only assign two or three. If students can correctly solve the problems assigned, they do not need to do more. If they struggle with the assigned problems, then the homework could point them to other specific problems in the problem set to help build their understanding. Offering problem solutions is also beneficial so that students do not need to wait until the next class period to learn whether their problem-solving approaches were successful.

HOW DO I CHOOSE WHAT TO ASSIGN FOR HOMEWORK?

As with any assignment, for best results carefully consider your learning goals and match them with the structure of the assignment. Here are some examples.

If you want students to . . .	. . . then they might do the following as homework
Observe natural phenomena outside the classroom	Journals Drawings Creating data tables Videos
Practice problem-solving	Problem sets Journals
Understand the connection between theory and practice in the lab	Lab write-ups with narrative Journals
Prepare for classroom discussion	Annotations of reading
Understand an idea from many examples	Video instruction
Project work	Narratives Presentation Graphs

The research also suggests that if you want students to practice skills, they must already have some competence in the skill before starting on the assignment (Cooper et al., 2006). Finally, make sure that your problem-solving ties to the standards and occurs on a need-to-know timeline. While we may want all students to have proficiency in calculations and quick recall of certain vocabulary and facts, these skills can be picked up during lessons as needed. They do not have to be acquired beforehand through any type of rote assignment.

HOW DO I GIVE FEEDBACK ON HOMEWORK?

One of the best ways to amplify learning is through feedback (see Feedback p. 142). As you assign homework, make sure to plan exactly how you will provide feedback. Consider the following questions:

- Will you provide commentary as students work on the assignment in class?
- Will you grade the assignment and write on the work?
- Will students self-grade according to a key?
- Will you use peer grading?

It helps if students are clear about the goal of feedback: *to help them improve*. Help them figure out what to do with the feedback they are given. Here are some actions that might follow an assignment that allows for improvement:

- Students resubmit a larger piece of work such as a lab report, addressing the feedback they were given. This can be as in depth as a rewrite or as simple as

Great Resources

Information on giving feedback on homework, https://bit.ly/3qWsEsb

annotations made by the student for each piece of written feedback received from the teacher.

- The teacher interviews a student about feedback given and asks what they might do differently or what they now know.

HOW DO I TREAT LAB WRITE-UPS?

Lab write-ups are standard practice for science courses because they are a great example of the practice of science: Find something out, then share it with others. Write-ups are often assigned as homework, but this can vary widely from teacher to teacher.

Here are some common challenges to lab write-ups and tips for feedback.

Challenge	Tip for Feedback
Students can go through a lab experience not really understanding what they are doing.	Give students an opportunity to write some narrative around their understanding of the ideas the lab is supposed to illustrate, which can be done before or after the actual time at the lab bench.
Students typically learn very little when they copy procedure instructions from their manual.	If the lab is one where the procedure is already determined, then the writing procedure is usually unhelpful. If the students need to *create* a procedure (e.g., "Determine a way to separate this sand and salt"), then having them write out the procedure is both instructive and helpful for assessment.
Students often don't know what good scientific documentation looks like.	Provide examples of the kind of write-up you are looking for. This can be done at the beginning of the year with a template. The quality of student write-ups improves dramatically when they have a quality example to model after.
Students aren't aware of how they will be assessed on a lab write-up.	Providing a rubric for the students sets clear expectations about what is expected and, depending upon the rubric, how they might improve.

See the science documentation template that follows.

Introduction:
• Does your introduction include information about why we've engaged in this course of study?
• What are the objectives of this investigation?
Prediction:
• Is your prediction based on past experience or sound reasoning?
• Will this investigation help you understand something about your prediction?
• Are all objectives addressed in your prediction?
Experiment/design procedure:
• If students are designing the experiment, this section could be included. If not, consider it optional.
• Does your design test all parts of your predictions?
• Are you taking enough data to test your prediction?
• Is your description clear enough that the experiment could be replicated by someone else?

<table>
<tr><td colspan="2">Data:</td></tr>
</table>

Data:

- Is it tabulated so that it is easy to understand?
- Are all data labeled, and do they have units? Advanced: Have you indicated error in your measurements?

Analysis:

- If your analysis requires calculation, are the calculations shown?
- If your analysis requires graphs, have you included them with all necessary labels, units, and titles?
- Have you addressed every part of your prediction?
- How do your findings compare to standard equations and/or theory?
- Have you discussed error in your measurements and calculations and how that error might limit your conclusions?

Summary:

- How do your results compare to your prediction?
- Have you included specific numbers and findings in your summary?

See sample rubric below.

Experiment/Lab Write-Up Rubric			
Section	**Unsatisfactory**	**Basic**	**Comprehensive**

Title/ introduction	• No title, or nonsensical title
	• Does not state all objectives
	• Incorrect grammar/ spelling
		• Title present
		• States what you will do in the lab
		• Uses complete sentences
			In addition to proficient descriptors:
			• Lab title clever, or uses appropriate humor
			• Introduction explains why objectives are worth studying by
			  • relating to real-world activities and/or
			  • relating to topics already studied, or to topics to be studied

Hypothesis	• No hypothesis stated • Does not address all objectives • Not testable • Incomplete sentences used	• All objectives of lab addressed by hypothesis • Testable hypothesis • Written in complete sentences	In addition to proficient descriptors: • Supports hypothesis with sounds reasoning or past experience
Experiment design/ procedure	• Experiment does not test hypothesis, or parts of hypothesis not addressed • Variable not controlled • Descriptions of procedure vague or difficult to follow	• Experiment tests the hypothesis • Design suggests enough data is gathered • Variables controlled • Written procedure allows for replication	In addition to proficient descriptors: • Written procedure includes diagrams/ photos • Design anticipates sources of error and attempts to minimize them
Data	• Absent • Numbers not labeled • Units missing some or all data	• Information in organized, easy-to-read format • Data labeled (e.g., time, velocity, etc.) • Units on data noted (e.g., seconds, m/s, etc.)	In addition to proficient descriptors: • If appropriate, data is organized in a table • Order that data appears in reflects the order in which it was gathered

(Continued)

MANAGEMENT

| Analysis | • Data that should be graphed is not
• Graphs incomplete
• Graphs not explained
• Calculations absent
• Values given without showing work
• Values missing units, or units incorrect
• Values incorrect
• Incorrect equations used
• Claims made without justification
• Claims made incorrectly
• No evidence of consideration of accepted values
• Error not discussed | • Appropriate graphs of data included
• Graphs complete (labels, units, title, curve-fit)
• Graphs accompanied by explanation of meaning
• Necessary calculations shown
• Calculations done correctly, with appropriate equation
• Calculated values have correct units, signs, etc.
• Answers to objectives are justified with scientific reasoning and with references to specific data and/or graphs
• Answers to objectives make sense based upon measurements and calculations
• Scientific reasoning correct
• Findings compared to theory, accepted values, or knowledge if appropriate
• Percentage error calculated
• Sources of errors mentioned | In addition to proficient descriptors:

• Analysis section organized and easy to follow
• Equations are derived, explained, and justified
• Calculations begin with general equation, show data plugged into equation, and then final answer very clearly shown
• Multiple calculated values organized, in a table if possible
• Calculations rounded to correct number of significant digits
• Research evident, quoted, and cited, and data based upon findings
• Demonstrates curiosity beyond scope of objectives and discusses possible directions for further experimentation
• Cause and effect of errors discussed, accompanied by calculations if possible |
| Summary | • Does not respond to all objectives/questions
• Does not discuss hypothesis
• Assessment of hypothesis incorrect or unreasonable
• Numerical values missing if called for in objectives | • Briefly states response to all objectives and questions
• Discusses validity of all hypotheses | In addition to proficient descriptors:

• Assessment of hypothesis correct
• Contains numerical values if called for in objectives |

WHAT ARE SOME DOS AND DON'TS OF ASSIGNING AND ASSESSING HOMEWORK?

Dos	Don'ts
Use homework as a reinforcement of ideas in the course.	Use homework as a punishment for bad behavior.
Help students keep their workload balanced by providing varied due dates.	Assign more than an hour of homework on any given night.
Provide some time in the classroom for engaging in homework so that you can provide real-time feedback.	Assign homework without making sure that students are super clear about the expectations.
Consider self-grading for homework. Studies show improved metacognition and achievement among students who self-graded some assignments (Handley et al., 2021).	Grade homework like a summative assessment. Students are often still formulating ideas.
Allow students to work together on homework.	Require students to work on all homework assignments alone.
Provide for differentiation opportunities. Some teachers might give students the choice of longer, slightly easier problem sets or shorter, more challenging ones.	Give the same assignment to all students.

Access and Equity

You may want to allow more time to complete assignments for students who take longer to process information. You also need to consider that not every student may have access to computers and the internet. You may want to consider providing opportunities at school to get online.

MANAGEMENT

HOW DO I ENGAGE MY STUDENTS IN SCIENCE?

The *Framework for K–12 Science Education* advocates for engaging students in doing science instead of having a teacher provide all the knowledge to students. According to the framework, there needs to be a transition from a "sit and get" classroom, where the teacher talks and students listen, to one where students talk and do science practices through the lens of a Crosscutting Concept (CCC) to learn. One of the ways to make this transition is through project-based learning (PBL), in which students work in groups to engage in the content of a defined problem. One Disciplinary Core Idea (DCI) outlined in the framework is Engineering, Technology, and the Application of Science. PBL allows students to work on solving problems like engineers do: using science ideas to design solutions.

Students will need to become critical thinkers to be engaged in science. This includes observing, finding problems, connecting, using flexible thinking, comparing and contrasting, evaluating, and interpreting using the Science and Engineering Practices (SEPs). Using these methods to evaluate claims in the media is especially important in today's world since findings often are not backed by empirical evidence in the popular press. As students become involved in these endeavors, they may experience frustration since they are not being told exactly what to do. Teachers can help by supporting productive struggle, which builds useful and lasting conceptual understanding and supports the development of critical-thinking skills.

Technology can help both teachers and students to engage in science. Teachers can use technology to track assessment and facilitate student interactions. Students can use technology for data-collecting analysis as they do SEPs to learn science ideas.

Each student has different strengths and areas where they need more work. They also have varying interests and experiences, so differentiation will need to be done to make science accessible for all students.

This chapter answers questions about how to engage students in science. These questions include the following:

- ☐ **How can I use PBL in the science classroom?**
- ☐ **What process can I use for teaching PBL?**
- ☐ **How do I teach problem-solving?**
- ☐ **How do I support my students in becoming critical thinkers?**

- ☐ **How do I promote and support productive struggle?**
- ☐ **How do I use technology?**
- ☐ **How do I provide differentiation for students?**

As you read about these topics, we encourage you to reflect on the following questions:

- ☐ **What does this mean to me?**
- ☐ **What else do I need to know about this?**
- ☐ **What will I do next?**

How Can I Use Project-Based Learning in the Science Classroom?

Many teachers have come to adopt PBL as a helpful pedagogy that encourages students to work in groups and engage in the content through an application or simulation that mirrors the work of the world outside the classroom. Science teachers are often more apt to take on PBL because they typically have a good understanding of the intersection between theory and application and they see that work on a project can build skills that scientists and engineers value.

WHAT IS PROJECT-BASED LEARNING?

Just because a learner is engaged in a project doesn't mean that PBL is happening. Let's distinguish doing projects from PBL.

When teachers do projects, the projects are often used as a replacement for a pencil-and-paper test or as an addition to the test done at the end of a unit. For example, a teacher teaching about parts of a cell might give some lectures, show some videos, and assign some reading, then later task the students with creating a poster that likens the cell to a city, with parts of the cell analogous to parts of the city. Note that the structure has the project coming at the end.

But this structure doesn't reflect what we know about how people learn. For example, if you have a leak in your roof, you might spend some time finding where the leak is coming from, then you might do research to find a good roofer, weigh the merits of you fixing the leak versus hiring a roofer to replace the roof, and learn about house construction in the process. Notice that the leak came first. Rarely do adults take classes in leak repair first and then wait until the class is over to be ready to deal with leaks.

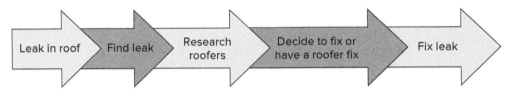

In PBL, rather than waiting until the end of the unit, a teacher will introduce a complex problem or phenomena first. The problem or task then creates the need to know something, and the content will support students in solving the problem. Instruction is couched as a means of helping the students solve the problem. To help with project management, teachers will often break up the project into distinct sections with benchmarks, particularly if the project is serving in place of a unit. Indeed, project planning is effectively unit planning (see Unit Planning p. 56).

Here's an example of a project plan.

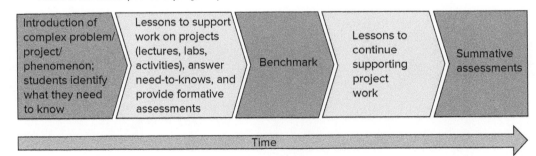

WHY DO PROJECT-BASED LEARNING?

Because in PBL students typically work in groups and communicate with each other, PBL gives students tangible longer-term engagements that allow them to understand the nuances of collaboration, communication, agency, and creativity. Students often create team documents, like contracts, that help them guide and maintain their long-term work, thus providing them the very valuable skill of project management.

PBL also encourages critical thinking. Because the world is complicated, PBL provides an opportunity to see how many ideas might fit together in more complex ways than a textbook might offer. A student might read about friction forces and calculate the coefficient of friction in a textbook, but in a project where students are understanding how skid marks on the road help them reconstruct a traffic accident, they must also take into account multiple tires, possible liquids or sand on the road surface, and so on.

PBL can get students out of the classroom and into the world where they gain practice speaking with experts, they see the overlap between ideas and complex systems, and they are able to exercise self-agency—all of which engage students and keep them motivated to learn.

HOW AUTHENTIC DO PROJECTS NEED TO BE?

When designing a project, a teacher must choose how authentic the project will be, which invokes a spectrum of possibility. On one end of the continuum, a teacher might have the students engage in a scenario that is hypothetical but mirrors the work of professionals, while on the other end might be a project where the work of the students is in fact used by professionals outside of school.

See the two examples of these approaches that follow to show projects that have actually been carried out in classrooms.

Scenario Driven	World Driven
Course: Biology	Course: Environmental science
Topic: Structure and function of cells	Topic: Biodiversity and local ecosystems
Students assume the role of doctor and are given a list of patients, each of whom has an illness that is associated with an organelle. In the final assessment, done as a simulation, students/doctors must determine the organelle associated with the illness and offer means of treatment.	The U.S. Department of Fish and Wildlife has acquired land that was formerly used for farming to create an urban wildlife refuge. Students are instructed to measure biodiversity in the area, assess the soil, and catalog current invertebrates in the area in preparation for land-forming that will happen as the land is transformed into the refuge.

When teachers take on PBL, they often start with scenario-driven projects because they can arrange the simulation to hit exactly the standards that they wish to cover, and the entire unit is often coordinated by the teacher, addressing particular standards in a specific order that the teacher determines. In a world-driven project, on the other hand, students might address a driving question in ways not anticipated by the teacher, and so the order of hitting standards might be more fluid. This fluidity requires that teachers understand how projects function so that they can meet students' needs flexibly. For that reason, world-driven sorts of projects are often done by more experienced PBL teachers.

Access and Equity

Considering the local community and its problems when planning PBL projects can provide a way that students can see how science relates to their lives. It is a valuable experience for all learners since it involves questions raised by students and is driven by their ideas for how to solve the problem. They feel ownership of the problem and can contribute to the learning process no matter what their language, whether or not they are neurodiverse, and regardless of their race, ethnicity, gender, and social economic status. All students can participate.

HOW DO EXPERIMENTS AND LAB EXPLORATIONS PLAY INTO PROJECT-BASED LEARNING?

As teachers think of applications for their projects, some have been tempted to eschew labs in favor of allowing more group time, practice for presentations, or any number of other project-oriented actions. We recommend that you follow your district's guidelines about time spent in investigations, which is often up to 40% of class time. This pushes the PBL teacher to incorporate labs into the project. Many science PBL teachers base their projects on these labs and create a narrative around the lab that includes a real-world context. For example, one teacher created a very simulation-oriented project where students played the role of engineers in gothic Europe, trying to understand how the Romans lifted heavy things. They carried out experiments determining the correct configuration of an effective pulley and carried out calculations around work to understand its efficiency. In another lab, students analyzed the pollution of a river, so they had to actually measure the water to determine pH, dissolved solids, and so on. Successful science PBL teachers use as much lab time as they can to reinforce the central ideas of the project.

Teaching in Flexible Settings

PBL can be successful in a hybrid setting. One of the first things to look at is what type of devices students have that will help them collect data and share their findings. Another consideration is finding a question that has students collaborate and share ideas both in and outside of school. It's important that all students have a voice in the question that is chosen. If you have some students in class and some working outside of school, you could pair students from these different locations together to collaborate.

EXAMPLES OF PBL PROJECTS

Subject	Big Ideas Addressed	Project
Biology	Photosynthesis, plant structure and function, biogeochemical cycles, human impact, amino acids, biotechnology, and climate change	**Meatless Mondays**: How can an environmental expo inform the public that small changes toward plant-based diets can have positive impacts on our climate?
Chemistry	Ionic bonds, molecular bonds, properties of ionic and molecular compounds	**Don't Sweat It**: Students develop a gel that allows a heart rate monitor to read on young kids, who don't sweat as much as adults. Final assessment includes a fund-raising walk and run where students use the gel.

(Continued)

Subject	Big Ideas Addressed	Project
Physics	Acceleration, velocity, projectile motion, forces	**Fireworks**: Students develop equations to describe when fireworks for a local July 4th display will reach their highest altitude, and they demonstrate their understanding of the fireworks as trajectories in a final presentation where they must calculate the landing spot of a projectile with a test in the classroom.

Great Resources

To learn more about PBL, see these resources:

- PBL resources collected by Edutopia, https://edut.to/3CIDEvL

- Rubrics to assess collaboration, communication, and agency from New Tech Network, https://bit.ly/3CHmgaz

- Video on the student-centered nature of PBL, https://youtu.be/ESFrPoZpKXQ

- Video explaining PBL, https://youtu.be/LMCZvGesRz8

- Video detailing five keys to PBL, https://youtu.be/hnzCGNnU_WM

- Projects from PBLWorks, https://my.pblworks.org/projects

- Blog by Kevin Gant exploring the landscape of PBL and instruction, https://intrepidedblog.wordpress.com/

What Process Can I Use for Teaching Project-Based Learning?

To get an idea of what a project process looks like, take a look at an example project. The steps in the project are presented in the order in which they would be performed in a classroom.

WHERE DO I START DEVELOPING A PROJECT?

Start with big ideas tied to the science standards of your state or the Next Generation Science Standards (NGSS). The big ideas and standards might look something like those in this table (which, as you'll see, fit the example project that follows).

Big Idea	Standards Related to the Big Idea
Gas solubility in water as a function of temperature	• The changes of state that occur with variations in temperature or pressure can be described and predicted using models of matter. (MS-PS1–4)
Local biomes	LS2.A: Interdependent Relationships in Ecosystems • Organisms, and populations of organisms, are dependent on their environmental interactions both with other living things and with nonliving factors. (MS-LS2–1) • In any ecosystem, organisms and populations with similar requirements for food, water, oxygen, or other resources may compete with each other for limited resources, access to which consequently constrains their growth and reproduction. (MS-LS2–1)
Different species of fish have different needs	• Growth of organisms and population increases are limited by access to resources. (MS-LS2–1)

WHAT ARE THE STEPS TO FACILIATING A PROJECT?

Here you'll see each section indicating a different step of the project. To the right is an explanation of the step.

Step 1: Entry Document	Explanation
Dear students, I am a landowner, and an avid snorkeler. I have an artesian well on my land, with beautiful clear water, and I would like to open it up to other snorkelers, but there are no fish in the well. I would very much like to know if there is enough oxygen in the water to support fish life in water of this temperature. If the well can support it, might you recommend at least four species of fish that will survive sustainably in the well, as well as native plant life I might plant around the well that can provide shade and a nice environment for visitors to picnic in?	An entry document can be a letter like this that starts a project. It lays out the task and gives some hints to the students about what content the project will include (for example "water of this temperature" and "native plant life"). Not all projects start with a letter—a project can be spurred by a guest speaker or a class discussion, for example—but there is always a written statement about the task that students can refer to over the course of the project.

Step 2: Know/Need to Know/Next Steps			
What Do We *Know*?	**What Do We *Need to Know*?**	**What Are Some *Next Steps* That We Might Take?**	**Explanation**
• Artesian well should support fish for snorkelers to see. • Need to find at least four species. • Need to determine something about oxygen in the water. • Must recommend plant life to provide a nice picnic area.	• What is the temperature of the water? • How do we determine oxygen levels in water? • What kinds of fish might survive in that environment? • How many of *those* fish would be cool to see as a snorkeler? • What kinds of plant life are used in local parks?	• Determine what an *artesian well* is. • Get temperature data from owner. • Look up the relationship between oxygen and water temp. • Look up fish species according to temperatures.	• This "knowing" document is created by the students and often facilitated by the teacher. After the entry event, students identify what they know about the project, what they don't know and therefore need to know, and, finally, what next steps they might take in order to accomplish the project. • If the teacher has written the task with sufficient hints, the need-to-know list can incite and drive instruction and activities during the project.

Step 3: Some Instructional Activities to Support the Project	Explanation
• Research time: Students act upon next steps • Group establishment: Writing group contract, setting goals, assigning roles (see Talk Formats p. 120; Differentiation p. 107) • Lab: What is the relationship between concentration of dissolved oxygen and water temperature? • Lecture: What is the solubility of gas in liquids other than water and in water? • Field trip to local body of water to measure dissolved oxygen • Pencil-and-paper quiz or test • Final presentation	These activities are often referred to as *scaffolds* because they help the students build their product step by step. There are multiple features to note: • Instruction in a project might look very much like traditional teaching. If, for example, a lecture is the most efficient way to communicate an idea, it is welcome in a project setting. While the means of instruction might be similar, sometimes the timing varies depending upon when students need the information. • There is an investigation in this project, which should always be the case in a science project. • There are two different means of summative assessment: both a pencil and paper quiz *and* a presentation. Formative assessment can take place throughout the project.

Step 4: Final Assessment Plan	Explanation
Quiz or test The quiz might look like a traditional quiz, asking students, for example, how to graph gas solubility in water versus water temperature, having them solve concentration problems, or questioning their understanding of which fish species live in various temperatures of water and biomes. **Presentation** Student groups present their findings to the teacher and invited guests—a snorkeler, a landscape designer, and a representative from the state's fish and wildlife department—all of whom use a rubric to assess the presentation.	While some PBL teachers prefer only performance-style assessments such as presentations, science teachers often need multiple means of assessing student knowledge. It is often helpful to provide a quiz before a presentation so that the presentation will be supported by better student knowledge.

HOW LONG WILL IT TAKE TO DO A PROJECT?

The project we just discussed is likely to take about two weeks of 50-minute class periods. One way to think about the length of the project is to consider how many lessons are required to answer the need-to-know list. Add to that number an introduction day, enough assessment days to accommodate all groups, a test day, and a couple of work days. If presentations are included, add two more days plus a day to roll out the project.

Notes

How Do I Teach Problem-Solving?

Teaching problem-solving in science courses requires using the SEPs to support students in reasoning about and understanding the conclusions they can draw from scientific data and evidence. While the approaches to problem-solving in science and engineering may be different, as we will discuss next, it is necessary for students to engage in this activity in order for them to make sense of science ideas.

WHAT IS THE DIFFERENCE BETWEEN SOLVING PROBLEMS IN SCIENCE AND IN ENGINEERING?

Scientists and engineers both solve problems. Scientists ask questions about the natural world to develop models and explain how things happen. Engineers also ask questions to define problems. Engineers then use science to design a solution to the problem. For example, scientists may determine the science behind how various minerals besides silica could transfer energy efficiently, while engineers would figure out how to use that information to design and build solar panels. Engineering involves criteria that are needed for a successful solution and considers what constraints there are for a specific task. It also involves seeking better, faster, and/or cheaper solutions to a problem. Science classes need to include activities to help students think about problems in the real world just like scientists and engineers do (see Practices p. 48).

HOW IS PROBLEM-SOLVING DONE IN SCIENCE?

Problem-solving in science involves using the SEPs to make claims that are backed by evidence (see Practices p. 48).

The following table shows how problem-solving compares in science and engineering.

Science Problem-Solving	Engineering Problem-Solving	Differences Between Problem-Solving Styles
Scientists make claims backed by evidence. Scientists • ask questions, • plan and conduct investigations, • analyze the evidence that they collect, • then argue with others about their models, questions, and explanations.	Engineers work with an engineering design process that guides them as they solve problems. Engineers • also plan and conduct investigations, analyze the evidence that they collect, and argue with others about their models, questions, and explanations, • always repeat steps, often more than once,	• Typically, scientists ask questions about the natural world and engineers ask questions related to problems they're trying to solve. • Although scientists usually construct explanations and engineers usually design solutions, they sometimes do both.

(Continued)

ENGAGEMENT

(Continued)

Science Problem-Solving	Engineering Problem-Solving	Differences Between Problem-Solving Styles
Scientists do not always do these practices in a particular order. They may go back and revisit and change a question, an investigation, a model, or an explanation.	• learn from their failures to design new and better solutions to the problem, • use the core ideas of science to advance their thinking, • can test their ideas before they research every aspect of their design, • redesign and try again.	• Engineers specify constraints and criteria for their solution. • Engineers can produce prototypes of the design they create.

In science and engineering, *argument* occurs when scientists listen to others as well as compare and evaluate different ideas based on evidence and reasoning. This process leads to explanations that are accepted by the scientific community and design solutions that are accepted by the engineering community. This is different from the use of *argue* in everyday language, which could carry a negative connotation.

There are people who think that students are solving problems when they are doing things like converting chemical formulas to the name of the compound, plugging numbers into an equation such as $F = ma$, or labeling the steps in mitosis. These are problems *associated* with science, but engaging in such activities gives a distorted view about doing science. Students who are asked to concentrate more on these types of problems in science class are less likely to see science as relevant to their lives and do not really understand how science is done. If we take away the SEPs from problem-solving and do not have students doing the questioning, figuring out, and making sense through the lenses of the CCCs, students do not gain a complete, coherent view of science. This type of science learning can cultivate attitudes towards science as a boring, irrelevant subject that has one right path to an uncontested answer. It is the job of science teachers to help students see that science affects their lives in many ways and is exciting and even fun to learn.

Likewise, it would be a good idea to avoid assigning an engineering problem that does not use the science ideas that have been learned by students. For example, having students participate in designing a way for an unbroken raw egg to be dropped from a height and not break might include discussion about reducing the amount of energy transformed from potential to kinetic energy, transferring the energy to a cushion around the egg, air resistance, and what happens when two objects collide. Just having students make a cushion for the egg without taking any of the science into account will not accomplish the objective of using science ideas to design a solution.

Try to help students to not just Google a solution to their problem and copy exactly what they find online. Engineers do research solutions, but they rely on a synthesis of ideas from many varied and reliable sources. Encourage students to try their own ideas. When their designs do not work as expected, help students see that it is essential to redesign and try again.

Great Resources

A detailed description of the differences between how scientists and engineers use the practices can be found at https://bit.ly/3XoLqof.

HOW DO I TEACH PROBLEM-SOLVING THROUGH AN ENGINEERING PROBLEM?

Great Resources

Teach Engineering at https://bit .ly/3pkCzaq offers many ideas about how to incorporate three-dimensional science learning and engineering.

1. Start students with an anchoring phenomenon. (For more about phenomena, see Unit Planning p. 56.) All of the sections of the design process can be revisited at any time to improve the solution. It is not a step-by-step linear procedure.

2. Next, ask students to define the problem. This involves identifying what they need to know, the materials available, and what constraints and limitations they must deal with. In a science class, limitations could be the size of the design, the materials used, or the cost. At this stage you want to ensure that the problem is related to the science concepts that you want students to include in their design and not just about the materials that they can use. This step can be done as a whole class or in groups. For example, if you want to have students design and build a bridge, you might tell them that they need to incorporate Newton's third law of motion and forces. It is important that the relevant science concepts be a part of their criteria and constraints.

3. Students can then research the problem in groups by looking for solutions that are already in use to determine what characteristics might be used from those designs. They also can figure out how the science ideas that they need to solve the problem work. Brainstorming possible ideas is important so that students have multiple ideas to choose from.

4. Finally, they can select a solution, make and test the solution, evaluate their solution, and then improve their design based on their findings.

During the design process, you can do some formative assessment by asking teams about their designs and how they incorporated the science concepts into their designs. Students sharing their final design with the class and explaining these ideas as well as how the process worked in their group is an important part of the experience.

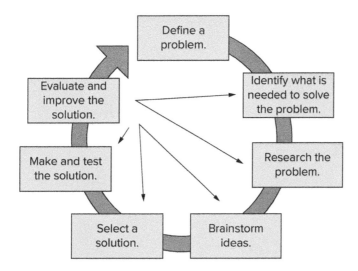

ENGAGEMENT

How Do I Support My Students in Becoming Critical Thinkers?

Critical thinking in science education involves "reflection on and evaluation of available evidence" (Wentzel, 2014, p. 579). Seven skills that are involved in critical thinking have been identified:

1. observing,
2. problem-finding,
3. connecting,
4. flexible thinking,
5. comparing and contrasting,
6. evaluation,
7. interpreting (Butcher et al., 2018; Butcher et al., 2017).

HOW CAN THREE-DIMENSIONAL LEARNING HELP STUDENTS LEARN CRITICAL THINKING?

The three dimensions of science—the DCIs, the SEPs, and the CCCs—help students learn critical thinking (see Three-Dimensional Learning p. 42 for more information). As students do the SEPs, they will develop skills that can help them be better critical thinkers. SEPs are practices that scientists and engineers use daily in their work and include the following:

- asking questions (for science) and defining problems (for engineering),
- developing and using models,
- planning and carrying out investigations,
- analyzing and interpreting data,
- using mathematics and computational thinking,
- constructing explanations (for science) and designing solutions (for engineering),
- engaging in argument from evidence,
- obtaining, evaluating, and communicating information.

(For more information, see Practices p. 48.)

By having students engage in the active investigation of a phenomenon and make sense of it, you are bringing out the following indicators of critical thinking.

Observation	Phenomena are observable events in our natural or designed universe. (For more about phenomena, see Unit Planning p. 56.) Because they know they'll need to make sense of a phenomenon, students pay careful attention.
Finding a problem	One of the central activities of both scientists and engineers, finding a problem issues directly from observations of interesting and/or odd phenomena. It gives students opportunities to reason about phenomena.
	Students then can plan and conduct an investigation to help explain how or why the phenomenon is happening.

(Continued)

Finding a problem (*Continued*)	This helps students see that they are doing science by making sense of the world around them and not just memorizing facts or doing a traditional lab by blindly following prescribed directions.
Connection	Exploring a phenomenon helps support students in critical thinking by forging connections between the science practices and the DCIs.
Interpret	After students gather data from investigations or look at data that has been collected by scientists in case studies, students need to be able to analyze and interpret the data.
	Since there are different ways that data can be analyzed, students can be given opportunities to look at the results of their classmates and respond.
Flexible thinking	Developing models and constructing explanations also lead to critical thinking as students think flexibly and come up with different models and explanations.
	Students are providing evidence for claims and reasoning to tie the evidence to the claim. They need to understand that, in science, claims must be backed by evidence.
Comparing and contrasting	Having students argue about their questions, data analysis, models, or explanations is one way to teach critical thinking since they are comparing and contrasting their ideas with those of others.
Evaluation	Students evaluate each other's ideas and communicate their findings. Coming to consensus as a class on the explanation for a phenomenon shows how science is done by professional scientists.

Connections also happen as teachers help students with the CCCs. The CCCs are ways of looking at a problem, especially if it is interdisciplinary, and include the following seven concepts:

1. patterns,
2. cause and effect: mechanism and explanation,
3. scale, proportion, and quantity,
4. systems and system models,
5. energy and matter: flows, cycles, and conservation,
6. structure and function,
7. stability and change.

(See Three-Dimensional Learning p. 42, for more information.) These concepts give students connections between disciplines in science so that they can, for example, see energy and matter in life science, physical science, Earth science, and engineering.

Great Resources

Data Nuggets (https://data nuggets.org/) give students the background about a scientist, their study system, and their research. Students interpret the real data and support their claims using the data as evidence.

HOW DO I TEACH STUDENTS TO USE CRITICIAL-THINKING SKILLS TO EVALUATE SCIENTIFIC CLAIMS IN THE MEDIA?

There is quite a bit of misinformation about science in the media, and with the increase of students' access to technology, students need to be able to discern science from opinion (and outright fabrication). It is very important to help students think critically as they evaluate claims that they hear, see, or read.

Here are a few tips for questions to share when students approach an article.

Tip 1   Ask: What is the purpose of the article?

Tip 2   Ask: Who wrote it and when was it written?

Tip 3   Ask: What are the author's claims and what is their evidence?

Tip 4   Ask: Who funded the study?

The most reliable scientific claims are made by recognized experts and based on recent scientific evidence. Students could examine the motivations behind the claims and think carefully about who sponsored the research. Let's put these tips into action using science reporting around climate change as an example.

Questions	Potential Response	Evaluation of Responses
What is the purpose of the article?	To persuade	Scientists publish the findings of their research to inform the public and other scientists of these findings. Such articles are not written as editorials that seek to persuade readers to think a particular way.
Who wrote it and when was it written?	Paid endorser, written 20 years ago	Students could be asked to look for up-to-date content written by scientific experts in peer-reviewed journals as the most reliable science content. Peer review is intended to weed out any data from experimentation that might not have been rigorous enough.
What are the authors' claims and what is their evidence?	The claim is that the science is uncertain.	The claim of "uncertain" science happens frequently with the science of climate change, even though 97% of climate scientists agree that climate change is happening and agree that it is primarily caused by emissions from human activities (Cook et al., 2016).
Who funded the study?	Oil and gas company	Instruct students to look for a hidden agenda when content is published by an organization that has much to gain financially (or much to lose).

As you can see from this example, one strategy that is used in the media to spread misinformation is to claim that the science is "uncertain." Sharing the existence of this technique with students and making them aware that there is consensus among scientists about climate change may help them consider evidence supporting these claims. Tobacco companies originally used this tactic in refuting the scientific claim that smoking causes cancer. They sowed doubt that the claims were valid, but many years later and after many deaths, the general public now agrees with the science linking smoking and cancer (Oreskes & Conway, 2010). This strategy has consequences, which can include lives lost and our home, the Earth, becoming irrevocably changed.

Identifying the source of the information is another technique to teach students to think critically. Just as the claims of "uncertain" science are used by oil and gas companies that stand to lose monetarily with a change in energy usage, the same doubt was used to make people feel okay about smoking. The opposite tactic is used in the sale of useless and sometimes harmful "health" products. Students can be taught how to look for evidence that claims are backed by scientific research rather than by those who stand to make a profit on the misinformation.

Teaching students how scientific consensus works can also help students think critically. They can see how scientific institutions such as the Intergovernmental Panel on Climate Change, the National Academies of Science, and the Centers for Disease Control bring together experts to evaluate scientific claims. Being experts, the members of these organizations have deep knowledge about the topics in their fields and argue their ideas to come up with the one that is best supported by the data. This can inspire confidence by the public in their claims.

How Do I Promote and Support Productive Struggle?

When we think of *struggle*, we think of great difficulty or effort. Struggle in the classroom can take many twists, and some may see struggle as a source of frustration for students. Likewise, students' struggles with learning may be viewed as a problem and often cast a negative or deficit light on the student (Hiebert & Wearne, 1993; Borasi, 1996). But here is the good news: Student struggle is productive! When we refer to *productive struggle*, we are talking about the process of effortful learning that develops persistence and supports creative problem-solving. Productive struggle goes beyond passive reading, listening, or memorizing and recalling. Productive struggle occurs when students labor and wrestle with ideas while making sense of the problem.

WHY IS PRODUCTIVE STRUGGLE IMPORTANT?

Research shows that productive struggle builds useful and lasting conceptual understanding and supports the development of critical-thinking skills (Hiebert & Grouws, 2007; see Critical Thinking p. 96). Neuroscientists have found that when the signals from a brain travel repeatedly through a nerve cell, a substance called myelin is produced. It makes brain signals faster and stronger, which is what happens when students are engaged in productive struggle (Sriram, 2020). Students are able to remember things for a longer time and apply ideas to a new situation when they figure things out on their own as compared to being told (Wirebring et al., 2015). When students work to define the problem, grapple with ideas, and are afforded the opportunity to come up with and reflect on their own solution pathways, they develop persistence and resilience in working toward their learning goals (Jackson & Lambert, 2010). With the help of the teacher, productive struggle can be fostered in students and contribute to positive and lasting learning outcomes.

Great Resources

A great resource demonstrating why it is important for scientists to fail and fail again can be found on the National Science and Technology Medals Foundation website at https://bit.ly/44gZgef.

HOW DO I PROMOTE PRODUCTIVE STRUGGLE?

When you model for your students that learning science is a space where ideas are shared, questioned, and revised in light of new evidence, you are illustrating to them that science is a place where we grapple with ideas to build an understanding. Welcoming and expecting students to share their reasoning and encouraging multiple representations of solution pathways promotes the process of productive struggle. It is important to teach early on that students are free to and encouraged to apply their own thought processes when faced with challenges. This sends the message that productive struggle is a mainstay in your science classroom.

The following are a few strategies and teacher moves to employ that support productive struggle:

- Share stories of how scientists productively struggle. It is rare that scientists get something right the first time.
- Provide time and opportunity for students to grapple with an idea, question, or solution pathway.

- Create tasks that have familiarity and draw on students' experiences and contexts.
- Provide time for reflection on group problem-solving.
- Use question techniques (see Facilitation p. 124) that:
  - ask students to explain their reasoning,
  - ask students to share why a strategy worked,
  - ask students to describe a different way to approach a problem.
- Model and establish norms that promote productive struggle.
  - Teach that being wrong is an opportunity to learn.

Great Resources

Visit
Mindresearch.org
for more detail on a few
teacher moves to try at
https://bit.ly/4416gws.

> When I started celebrating mistakes as an opportunity to learn during warm-ups, students were more willing to try new ways of thinking about a problem and share that with the class.

—HIGH SCHOOL CHEMISTRY TEACHER IN CALIFORNIA

Here are some dos and don'ts to help avoid students shutting down during productive struggle.

Dos	Don'ts	Why?
Praise students for persevering through a problem.	Praise students for being quick and fast and sharing correct solutions without reasoning.	Reasoning is essential for student understanding, so taking time for this is important. Rushing through a problem does not promote understanding.
Allow all students the time and space to discover problem-solving.	Give easier work to struggling students.	Providing a challenging and safe learning environment will give students the opportunity for productive struggle. By giving them time, they can problem-solve and feel satisfaction that they have achieved instead of easily coming up with an answer.
Display work that shows creative problem-solving.	Always display work that shows the highest scores.	Problem-solving is a mainstay in science. There are different ways to solve problems, so plan on recognizing students for creative ways they've approached problems.
Call on students who volunteer to answer but may not have the correct answer. You could also notify students who are reluctant to answer ahead of time that they will be called on to answer a specific question.	Always call on students who know the right answer.	To provide equity, try not to always call on students who always raise their hand and know the answer. But be aware that calling on students who do not have their hand raised may cause anxiety.

(Continued)

ENGAGEMENT

(Continued)

Dos	Don'ts	Why?
Give students informative feedback that helps them see how to find the answer themselves.	Assess student responses as right or wrong without having them figure out why they are right or wrong.	Encourage students to figure out an answer on their own and not just be told what the answer is. This helps them to more deeply understand and remember longer.
Allow time for students to tinker with ideas. Go slow to go fast.	Follow a strict schedule for covering new material.	Students need time to process and figure out how something works. You can evaluate formative assessment and see whether to move forward or revisit a concept.
Provide nonroutine problems that can't be solved with a memorized formula.	Provide problems that students can answer by using a formula without understanding the underlying concept.	Just filling in the blanks of a formula and getting the correct answer does not guarantee understanding.
Encourage a growth mindset. (See Narratives p. 25)	Think of students as having a fixed mindset where change is not possible.	Students can improve if they have time and put forth effort and practice. Teachers can help students think that this is possible.

I often tell my students: "I am going to tell you what
to do. I am not going to tell you how to do it."

—PHYSICS TEACHER FROM NEW MEXICO

Notes

How Do I Use Technology?

A science teacher has many options when it comes to implementing technology, the machinery and equipment that was developed for sharing scientific knowledge. This technology ranges from smartphones and Wi-Fi to sophisticated statistical software. Since many students were not in the classroom during the COVID-19 pandemic, a coordinated effort was made for students to have access to technology when they were studying remotely. There was inequity across the country with regards to this access, but funding was increased to address at least some of these problems. Although inequities still exist, more students have access to technology in the classroom than before the pandemic. In thinking about this, consider the areas where other teachers use technology:

- creating assessments and tracking grades,
- laboratory data collection and research,
- data analysis,
- facilitating student interactions.

WHAT ARE SOME TIPS FOR CREATING ASSESSMENTS AND TRACKING GRADES WITH TECHNOLOGY?

What software is used for tracking grades and storing/distributing written materials is often a decision made at the school level (rather than the science department), so consider speaking to your school administration about what is available to you. Because online grades are a way to keep students and their caregivers apprised of their progress in the course, it is a good idea to establish and clearly communicate your policies around posting grades. Placing your policies into a syllabus can make your communications with families predictable. If you are a new teacher, we recommend that you give yourself plenty of time to grade student work, but try to provide this feedback in a timely manner.

Great Resources

While all grades are the result of assessment, not all assessments require a grade. Sometimes an online source such as those listed below can help you quiz and assess the students, and can also help the students assess themselves.

- Plickers, https://www.plickers.com/
- Blooket, https://www.blooket.com/
- Kahoot, https://kahoot.com/
- Quizlet, https://quizlet.com/
- Nearpod, https://nearpod.com/

Great Resources

An excellent free source for using phones can be found at https://bit.ly/43TTyzr, a site hosted by Lawrence Livermore National Labs.

HOW CAN I USE TECHNOLOGY FOR INVESTIGATIVE DATA GATHERING?

Particularly if you are doing work on motion and forces, there are excellent motion-detecting devices available from the big catalogs—Flinn, Ward's, PASCO, and so on. The ability to gather and immediately show position, velocity, and acceleration with respect to time helps students see the connections between all three actions clearly.

In general, consider using digital devices when you want more detailed data. While an analog thermometer is helpful for a general picture of temperature, a digital thermometer can show you the smooth transitions of temperature over time, which is helpful for explorations around cooling or heating rates.

Spreadsheets are a great way for students to share and coalesce data from different groups. For example, you might have students determining river depth up and down a half mile of a river. Each group can upload their information to a single spreadsheet that all can use to create an overall understanding of the river.

Don't eschew the opportunities for students to use their own technology if they have it. Smartphones can be excellent video cameras and can also be programmed to take time-lapse photography. They also have built-in sensors that can help students collect motion data.

HOW CAN TECHNOLOGY HELP WITH ONLINE RESEARCH?

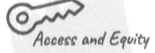

Access and Equity

While there are many labs that could benefit from the use of students' personal devices such as tablets, calculators, or smartphones, not all students have access to these items. To address this during investigations, you can ensure that all students are using school-issued tools (e.g., tablets, Chromebooks, timers, calculators) so as to reduce the chance of highlighting this difference.

Sometimes you would like students to research questions on the internet, which can be tricky, for obvious reasons. Here are three ways to structure research so that the students are on task, going to appropriate websites, and getting the information you want them to get.

1 **Pairing students**
Even if you have a 1:1 student-to-computer ratio, consider having students pair up with a single computer. This keeps both students more accountable and allows students to make sense of information together. Two people can view the same computer; more than two tends to leave a person out.

2 **Facilitated research time**
- Students are paired up and ready to go with a computer.
- Teachers or students provide a research question. Or groups could have a set of multiple questions that everyone needs to answer.
- Students research for a limited, timed duration. Typically it is short—five to ten minutes
- Share out. The teacher calls on various groups. Each group shares questions, information they found, and the website they investigated. This is a good time for the teacher to ask the rest of the class, "What do you think of the trustworthiness of this site?" (See Critical Thinking p. 96.)
- Groups go into another five-to-ten-minute research period.
- Groups share out again.
- Repeat as necessary. Three rounds is often adequate.

3 **WebQuest**

This is one of the first ideas that internet-savvy educators used in the late 1990s, but it is still very effective, particularly for younger students. The idea is that you create a task for students to accomplish, and then provide a series of sites—*and only those sites*—that the students can visit for research. Because this idea is older, relative to the internet, there are many WebQuests referenced that have links that no longer work. You will likely need to create your own and revisit the links regularly.

HOW CAN TECHNOLOGY HELP WITH DATA ANALYSIS?

There are many technology products that can be used for data analysis. The table below discusses the pros and cons of each product listed.

Product	Pros	Cons
Spreadsheet (such as Excel or Google Sheets)	• Can be free • Wide spectrum of commands makes it flexible • Excellent for statistical analysis • Integrates easily with documentation and presentation software • Many options for data sorting	• Less obvious to create *x-y* plots. • Difficult to use for best-fit lines and curve fitting
Data analysis software, such as Logger Pro (Vernier) or DataStudio (PASCO)	• Built for *x-y* plots • Excellent for curve fitting and creating best-fit lines • Often designed to communicate directly with sensors	• Fewer options for data sorting • Not as flexible with text • Can be expensive

WHAT TECHNIQUE CAN I USE TO HELP STUDENTS DOING ONLINE RESEARCH?

Here are some student-centered teaching techniques and some online resources that can help you facilitate when your students are online.

Teaching Technique	Online Resource That Helps	Video Description/Example
Lecture Presentation Socratic Seminar	• Any online video sharing	• Zoom • Microsoft Teams • Google Meet
Card sort	• Trello • Jamboard • Microsoft Visio • Miro	• Jamboard for card sort: https://bit.ly/3JXK4LN • Trello for card sort:https://bit.ly/406ZLWO

(Continued)

ENGAGEMENT

(Continued)

Teaching Technique	Online Resource That Helps	Video Description/Example
Jigsaw	• Zoom • Microsoft Teams • Using breakout rooms	
Concept mapping	• MindMup 2: https://www.mindmup.com/	• MindMup for concept mapping:https://bit.ly/3FHjJiG • Google Draw
Chalk Talk	• Padlet • ECHO discussion boards • Google Docs	• Padlet for Chalk Talk: https://bit.ly/3yViJni • Padlet in general: https://bit.ly/3JZzWSS
Concept attainment (a technique that uses examples and nonexamples as a way for students to construct a concept)	• Zoom, GoogleMeets, etc., if you want to do it live. • You can also provide this on a digital document or presentation software to list the examples and nonexamples.	• One online description of concept attainment with examples can be found at Cult of Pedagogy: https://bit.ly/42rd7xq
Labs	• Lots of ideas and online sources described at 10 Virtual Lab Activities to Try With Your Interactive Projector: https://bit.ly/3MZqLCn	
4 Corners	• Jamboard • Trello • MicroSoft Visio • Miro	• Jamboard for 4 Corners: https://bit.ly/3ndNgKF
Video journaling/discussion Project presentations	• Flip	
Student/teacher peer review and presentation Interactive video commenting	• VoiceThread	

Notes

How Do I Provide Differentiation for Students?

Each student has different strengths and also areas where they need more work. They have different interests and experiences. Standards that incorporate three-dimensional learning are for all students, so some differentiation will need to be done by the teacher so that every student can succeed. The learning goal is the same for all students, but the ways the teacher may provide to students to reach the goal will vary. Next, let's look at strategies for differentiation when teaching phenomenon-based lessons, in reading and writing in science class, in discourse, and in grouping.

You may want to think about the metaphor of windows and mirrors (Bishop, 1990) as you incorporate differentiation into your classroom. Windows are a metaphor for helping students to see a new perspective. The differences among students offers a unique opportunity for a teacher to highlight a range of experiences and understandings about a concept or idea. It is important to validate these perspectives and ideas and see them as a tool for developing greater understanding in your classroom. Mirrors help students to see what they already know. Providing examples of science professionals that look and act like them help them to see that people from their gender, racial group, or culture have contributed to science, that there are interesting perspectives raised by people who look like them, and ultimately that *they* are capable of succeeding in science no matter what career path they choose.

HOW CAN I USE DIFFERENTIATION WITH PHENOMENON-BASED LESSONS?

Here are some ideas about using differentiation in phenomenon-based lessons.

Type of Differentiation	Description
Share common experiences	Phenomenon-based lessons • allow students to share common experiences, • use different ways to learn, including kinesthetic, verbal, tactile, and visual, • are accessible for students with a range of learning preferences and language abilities,
Notice and wonder	Sharing noticings and wonderings about a phenomenon can lead to a class-identified question and provide extension activities for further investigation/research.
Elicit prior knowledge	Finding out what students already know related to the phenomenon may help you to address any alternative conceptions or tie in related student knowledge as students grow in their understanding of how the phenomenon works.
Investigate topics of interest	Students can be encouraged to investigate topics of interest to them that are related to the phenomenon as a way to increase motivation and agency.

(Continued)

ENGAGEMENT

Type of Differentiation	Description
Use of authentic assessments and projects	Authentic assessments that are focused on phenomena support understanding and coherence and offer opportunity to demonstrate the SEPs in many ways.
Low floor, high ceiling tasks	Phenomenon-based lessons provide low floor, high ceiling tasks. These are tasks that are accessible for all students but that can be taken to higher levels. (See Notes p. 145 for an example of a low floor, high ceiling task.)
Give a choice in assignments	When using problem sets, consider • offering longer problem sets so students have more practice opportunities, • using shorter, more difficult problem sets as a mini-summative assessment for students, • allowing students to choose the assignment they do.

HOW CAN I USE DIFFERENTIATION WITH READING AND WRITING IN SCIENCE?

Here are some ideas about using differentiation in phenomenon-based lessons.

Access and Equity

If you are working with multilingual learners or those who have physical or intellectual challenges, you may need to develop an interactive word wall. Consider including your class vocabulary in different languages, including braille. Make sure that text is large enough to be read from anywhere in the room. If possible, you could create your word wall on a mobile whiteboard or virtually so that it can be removed or covered during assessments when use of vocabulary is being tested.

Type of Differentiation	Description
Reading the most important parts of a text	Teach students to identify the most important parts of a reading and to skim, highlight, and rephrase to share their understanding. (They can still read the entire section if they want). You can also point them to those sections explicitly.
Follow up with sense-making questions	Help students to use questions to determine what they need to understand. Sense-making questions support synthesis and application of ideas rather than recall.
Word wall	List words on a word wall for students to refer to so that there is common language. This provides a consistent cue about new vocabulary.
Read/speak aloud	Having students read their own writing aloud can help them revise their argument and include any unintended omissions. This strategy can also be useful for students who need help scribing their work.
Introducing vocabulary words	Introduce vocabulary words when students need to know them as they complete a task. Front-loading all vocabulary at the beginning of a task can be daunting for many students.
Multiple means of representation	Let students represent their understanding in multiple ways and not just in text. For example, one student might write their understanding while another student might record it on their phone, and yet another might use a graph or draw their understanding.
Scaffolding	One way to scaffold is to give a clear explanation using multiple modes of communication, such as pictures and drawings. Graphic organizers can help focus thinking. Not all students require the same scaffolds. If there is choice in scaffolds, then you could instruct students on how to choose them.

HOW CAN I USE DIFFERENTIATION WITH DISCOURSE IN THE CLASSROOM?

See Chapter 4 about student talk in science (p. 112).

Here are some ideas about using differentiation in discourse.

Type of Differentiation	Description
Thinking time	Using think time gives all students a chance to formulate a response and figure out how to articulate it. This may be especially important for students who are English-language learners (ELLs) or learning disabled (LD), or who have auditory-processing difficulties.
Telling students ahead of time which question they will answer	Front-loading questions that students will answer gives them more time to formulate an answer. This is also a helpful technique in project-based learning. You can give some students the entry document/assignment the day before you roll it out with the entire class or share the question on a slip of paper or sticky note.
Think-Pair-Share	Have students think about their answer, share their ideas with a partner, then share with a group, and finally share with a whole classroom. This promotes equity of voice for all students.
Variety of ways to communicate ideas	Students may communicate better using certain methods. These could include text, talk, gestures, drawings, video recordings, and graphs.
Sentence starters	These could be posted on the wall, taped to the desk, or found in every student's notebook. This helps them to figure out ways to respond to or elicit ideas from other students in the classroom.
Dialogue protocols	Having dialogue protocols helps students to know how to contribute in a group. This helps those who may have difficulty in auditory processing or who are anxious about sharing. They have a specific protocol to follow and do not need to figure out what to do on their own. (See discussion of the Say Something Protocol in Facilitation p. 124.)

HOW CAN I USE GROUPING AS A DIFFERENTIATION TOOL?

See Grouping p. 74.

Here are some ideas about using differentiation in grouping.

Type of Differentiation	Description
Group students who are able to combine complex ideas that they have learned. This can be determined by formative assessment before the task.	If there are students who have shown by formative assessment to have an ability to combine complex ideas about a specific phenomenon, you may want to group them together and assign an application that is more complex.

(Continued)

ENGAGEMENT

(*Continued*)

Type of Differentiation	Description
Phenomenon probe	This will help to indicate alternative conceptions and prior knowledge. Differentiation can happen when students are assigned a group with students who have answers that are different than their answer. They can argue their ideas with others based on evidence. Lessons that help them understand why some of the answers are not scientifically accurate could follow their initial discussion.
Student interest and choice	It helps form a more cohesive group when groups are differentiated by interest and can choose what problem they want to solve and how to solve it.
Group roles	Provide roles for students in their groups based on their strengths. These roles could include resources manager, clarifier/facilitator, data recorder, questioner, reporter, devil's advocate/skeptic, teacher liaison, prioritizer/ progress monitor, checker, and timekeeper (see Talk Formats p. 120).
Grouping ELL students	When differentiating for ELLs, you may want to consider the following grouping structures: • *Group of all ELL students.* This might allow for the most free-flowing conversation and is especially useful in classrooms with multilingual teachers. • *Group with two ELL students and one English-language speaker.* This can support exchange of ideas if one or both of the ELL students have acquired sufficient language skills to communicate about the science ideas with students who don't speak another language.

Notes

chapter
FOUR

HOW DO I HELP MY STUDENTS TALK ABOUT SCIENCE?

Talking about science is an integral part of "doing science." Current reforms such as the Next Generation Science Standards specifically ask students to argue from evidence, develop and critique models, and share explanations. These science practices require students to develop and communicate ideas with one another in ways that mirror how scientists work together to build an understanding of the natural world. Providing opportunities for students to talk about the ideas they are developing is an effective student-centered way to teach science.

Supporting a student-centered classroom requires teachers to shift their stance from being one who offers up explanations to one who facilitates learning conversations. While students are adept at conversing in everyday life, they might find it difficult to draw from, use, and apply their lived experiences when talking about science in the classroom. Engaging in talk in the science classroom may feel unnatural for students because of a history of limited opportunities to freely share and interject ideas, describe their thinking, and actively listen to the ideas of others.

Effective teachers ensure that students get opportunities to talk about science. Supporting student talk in science requires planning for classroom discourse, choosing talk formats to meet the targeted learning goals you have for your students, using monitoring tools to gather data on the talk, and implementing classroom norms that support equitable participation in talk.

This chapter answers the following questions about how to help your class talk about science:

- [ ] **How do I plan for classroom discourse?**
- [ ] **How do I facilitate different types of conversations?**
- [ ] **How do I choose talk formats?**
- [ ] **How do I monitor classroom talk?**

As you read about these topics, we encourage you to reflect on the following questions:

- [ ] **What does this mean to me?**
- [ ] **What else do I need to know about this?**
- [ ] **What will I do next?**

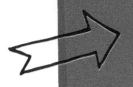

How Do I Plan for Classroom Discourse?

There are numerous possibilities for students to engage in talk in the science classroom. Planning for student talk begins with believing all students are capable of engaging in productive talk, setting a clear purpose for talk, and providing well-established structures of support for talk.

Identity & Agency

All students do not have the same cultural expectations of talk. For example, in some student homes co-talking or overlapping talk is the norm, while in other homes *one mic* or single speaker at a time is the norm. Understanding what is common among students at home or in friend groups is important so that you can figure out what ground rules need to be laid to best support the talk you want to cultivate. In addition, students who are learning academic English may engage in conversation more slowly or hesitantly. Employing active listening strategies can support all students in feeling safe to enter and engage in conversations.

- **Believe in students.**
  - Begin with a belief that all students are capable of engaging in productive talk; this will help you to approach classroom discussions with an asset perspective.
  - All students are capable of contributing to discussions, and the discussion itself serves as a place where sense-making skills are developed. But be patient: Not all students gain confidence in talking about science at the same pace.
- **Set clear expectations.**
  - Set a clear vision of the academic purpose for talk in supporting discourse in the classroom.
  - Understanding the core idea that is the focus of a task, how that idea relates to prior learning, and how it contributes to future endeavors is important in discerning the purpose for talk, and ultimately this guides the types of discussions you want students to engage in.
- **Build ground rules and support.**
  - Build well-established ground rules and scaffolded support to lay a foundation that creates a safe and inviting space for conversations.
  - Students must feel a sense of safety and trust that their ideas will be listened to, taken seriously, and handled with respect. Ground rules ensure that the ideas are welcomed and challenged and that the ideas and reasoning process are central. Ground rules protect speakers from being targeted when making their ideas public. These are important conversations to have with your students at the start of the school year (see Start of the Year p. 34).

Teaching in Flexible Settings

If you are teaching in a hybrid setting, there are ways that tech can support students in learning to listen and slowing down the conversation. For example, classes that meet on a virtual platform can benefit from all students except for the speaker being muted. The time it takes to unmute to add to a conversation can be experienced as wait or listening time for the speaker.

HOW DO I ANTICIPATE WHAT STUDENTS WILL DO AND SAY?

We want classrooms where students are making their observations and ideas public and they build off of each other's ideas. We also want students to develop flexibility and facility in engaging in the science practice of obtaining, evaluating, and communicating information (see Practices p. 48). Anticipating how students will communicate ideas before the lesson allows you to be better prepared and not feel like you are caught off guard. It also saves time spent in class processing what students are saying and what your response will be because you have already anticipated the possibilities. Anticipation also gives you confidence in the scientific ideas that are being developed because you have done this work ahead of time.

Anticipating helps you to think about the DCIs (see Three-Dimensional Learning p. 42) you want to build and the many different pathways your students might take to develop those concepts. As you think about the different ways ideas can be shared and revised in your classroom, consider the following strategies:

- Work with other teachers and look at other resources, both physical and virtual, to cast a wider net for different phenomena and associated storylines to build DCIs.
- Include misconceptions as well as productive pathways (see Productive Struggle p. 100). This will help you think about how to use misconceptions to the advantage of both you and your students.
- Plan questions you want to ask to assess and push each student or group's thinking.
- Think about connections between previous ideas and future goals so that you can remind students of prior knowledge and experiences that they can draw on to prompt future questions.

Once you have anticipated what students will do, you are now poised to plan for classroom discourse.

HOW DO I PLAN FOR CLASSROOM DISCOURSE?

As you think about and plan for talk in your classroom, consider the following strategies.

Set the Purpose for Talk 〉 Provide the Support for Talk 〉 Define the Outcome of Talk 〉

To illustrate each of these strategies, we share an example lesson that addresses NGSS MS Disciplinary Core Idea LS2.A: Interdependent Relationships in Ecosystems (Figures 4.1 and Figure 4.2) and the accompanied performance expectations (MS-LS2-4).

Great Resources

A valuable tool for thinking about anticipating, sequencing, connecting, and monitoring student ideas is *5 Practices for Orchestrating Productive Task-Based Discussions in Science* by Jennifer Cartier, Margaret Schwan Smith, Mary Kay Stein, and Danielle Ross.

Great Resources

Talk Activities Flowchart, https://stemteachingtools.org/sp/talk-flowchart

DISCUSSION

Figure 4.1 NGSS MS disciplinary core idea LS2.A

Disciplinary Core Ideas

LS2.A: Interdependent Relationships in Ecosystems

- Organisms, and populations of organisms, are dependent on their environmental interactions both with other living things and with nonliving factors.
- In any ecosystem, organisms and populations with similar requirements for food, water, oxygen, or other resources may compete with each other for limited resources, access to which consequently constrains their growth and reproduction.
- Growth of organisms and population increases are limited by access to resources.

Source: Next Generation Science Standards

Figure 4.2 Performance expectations MS-LS2

MS-LS2   Ecosystems: Interactions, Energy, and Dynamics

Students who demonstrate understanding can:

MS-LS2-1.   Analyze and interpret data to provide evidence for the effects of resource availability on organisms and populations of organisms in an ecosystem. [Clarification Statement: Emphasis is on cause and effect relationships between resources and growth of individual organisms and the numbers of organisms in ecosystems during periods of abundant and scarce resources.]

MS-LS2-2.   Construct an explanation that predicts patterns of interactions among organisms across multiple ecosystems. [Clarification Statement: Emphasis is on predicting consistent patterns of interactions in different ecosystems in terms of the relationships among and between organisms and abiotic components of ecosystems. Examples of types of interactions could include competitive, predatory, and mutually beneficial.]

MS-LS2-3.   Develop a model to describe the cycling of matter and flow of energy among living and nonliving parts of an ecosystem.

[Clarification Statement: Emphasis is on describing the conservation of matter and flow of energy into and out of various ecosystems, and on defining the boundaries of the system.] [Assessment Boundary: Assessment does not include the use of chemical reactions to describe the processes.]

MS-LS2-4.   Construct an argument supported by empirical evidence that changes to physical or biological components of an ecosystem affect populations. [Clarification Statement: Emphasis is on recognizing patterns in data and making warranted inferences about changes in populations, and on evaluating empirical evidence supporting arguments about changes to ecosystems.]

MS-LS2-5.   Evaluate competing design solutions for maintaining biodiversity and ecosystem services.* [Clarification Statement: Examples of ecosystem services could include water purification, nutrient recycling, and prevention of soil erosion. Examples of design solution constraints could include scientific, economic, and social considerations.]

The performance expectations above were developed using the following elements from the NRC document *A Framework for K-12 Science Education*:

Source: Next Generation Science Standards

HOW DO I DETERMINE THE LESSON SEQUENCE?

Let's take a look at a lesson.

1. Students are presented with a phenomenon of reproductive failure in common seabirds.

On the isle of Shetland (see Figure 4.3) off the coast of Scotland, there once were more than 1,200 nesting pairs of common murres (see Figure 4.4). In recent summers, there were none. The birds returned to their cliffside nesting grounds, but their nests remained empty. Elsewhere on Shetland, more than 20,000 nests of another seabird, the arctic tern, were vacant. And a few miles away, on the island of Foula, the largest colony in the world of great skuas had only a few chicks. Ornithologists say they have never seen such reproductive failure. It has resulted in the loss of hundreds of thousands of the world's seabirds (Dybas, 2006).

Figure 4.3 The Shetland Islands	Figure 4.4 The common murre seabird

Source: Moorefam/istock.com	*Source:* Frank Fichtmüller/istock.com

2. Students were provided an opportunity to define the problem, propose initial ideas, and come to a consensus on the driving question: Why is the common murre population declining?

3. Students were placed in groups. Each student in the group read a different article that detailed an aspect of the seabirds' biology. The four articles included information about the seabirds' feeding, mating-to-hatching period, life after hatching, and migration and movement. While reading, students were asked to annotate the text by highlighting things that were surprising, underlining important ideas, and putting parentheses around things they had questions about.

> Set the Purpose for Talk

Talk has many purposes in the science classroom. Whether the purpose is to surface prior knowledge, share observations, critique the reasoning of others, or offer an explanation, it is important to align the purpose of talk to the learning goal of the task. Task and talk alignment offers students the opportunity to use talk as a tool to develop a repertoire of critical-thinking skills (see Critical Thinking p. 96). Purposeful talk pushes students beyond simply recalling or reporting out toward developing *talk moves* that offer them the facility to engage in the Science and Engineering Practices (see Practices p. 48) to develop critical-thinking skills (see Critical Thinking p. 96). These skills support students to build, challenge, and revise the ideas that are the target of your instruction.

HOW DO I DETERMINE THE LEARNING GOAL OF THE LESSON SEQUENCE?

If we look back at our seabird example, the goal of reading and annotating the text was to provide each student with an opportunity to bring new and unique information to the table to influence the group's understanding of the seabird and its relationship to its environment. To realize that goal, students in the group must have a way to engage in conversation about what they learned from the text. The purpose set for the talk is to give students an opportunity to use what they read to express ideas, gain ideas, make connections among ideas, ask questions, make inferences, and modify their thinking to build an understanding of how the physical and biological components of an ecosystem affect populations.

> Provide the Support for Talk

Providing support for the purpose of talk can take many forms, such as protocols, sentence stems, or talking sticks, to name a few. In the seabird lesson, it was important for students to be able to bring unique information from their reading to the group. The group also needed structures to respond to that information in ways that offered clarifications, questions, and

Great Resources

A close-read protocol can support students in learning how to read and draw information from texts. You can modify a protocol like the one at https://bit.ly/480xXXQ.

opportunities to build on others' ideas. Protocols are good tools of support that can help students guide their conversations in small groups with a particular focus in mind. The Say Something Protocol offers scaffolded support to move students beyond engaging in a report-out style conversation to one that prompts them to actively reason with the ideas they are sharing. This protocol supports small groups in eliciting prior knowledge, putting ideas on the table, making connections, making inferences, and asking questions. It is carried out as follows:

1   The first person in the group shares their key point.
2   The next person in the group is the responder.
   - The responder, using the sentence starters shown in the table that follows, chooses to engage one of the following ways:
      - makes an observation,
      - clarifies something,
      - makes an inference,
      - makes a connection,
      - asks a question.

Sentence Starters for Say Something Protocol				
Observation	Clarification	Inference	Connection	Question
• I noticed that . . . • I think that . . . • I saw (heard, smelled) . . . • This is good because . . . • This is hard because . . . • This is confusing because . . . • This makes sense because . . .	• Now I understand . . . • No, I think it means . . . • At first, I thought . . . , but now . . . • I agree with your idea, and . . . • What this means is . . .	• I predict that . . . • I bet that . . . • Based on these data, I think . . . • One thing I am thinking is . . . • I wonder if . . .	• This reminds me of . . . • The process is like . . . • This is similar to . . . • This . . . makes me think . . . • This . . . is like . . . because . . .	• How did . . . ? • In what ways are . . . like . . . ? • Do you think that . . . ? • What evidence supports . . . ? • In other words, are you saying . . . ?

3   The responder then shares their key point and the next person in the group becomes the responder. This continues until all have shared at least two rounds of key points.

Here are a few tips to get you started with the Say Something Protocol.

Tip 1   Hand out laminated protocol cards for each group

Tip 2   Provide laminated sentence starter cards and have the students circle the ones they used

Tip 3   Place a physical copy of the sentence starters in a public place that is visible to students

> Define the Outcome of Talk

Defining the outcome of the talk aids you in planning for how you will monitor your students' progress. Information about how students are meeting your learning goal can help you understand how the supports you put in place are working for your students. In the seabird case, the product or outcome of the students' conversation about the readings led to the inclusion of new biotic and abiotic features in the revised model for the common murre's place within the ecosystem and supported students in developing an argument from evidence about how changes to the physical or biological components of an ecosystem affect populations. Identifying the ways students' conversations will be evident in the outcomes of learning helps you to understand how the talk contributed to your students' success in reaching the learning goal.

Tip Provide students with an exit ticket to reflect on their participation in the conversation with sentence starters: I learned _____ from listening to _____ about _____.

Great Resources

Success in Science Through Dialogue, Reading and Writing by Arthur Beauchamp, Judi Kusnick, Rick McCallum, and Jim Hollander provides protocols for productive dialogue, purposeful reading, and meaningful writing.

DISCUSSION

How Do I Choose Talk Formats?

Talking with another person about science ideas is complex and requires practice. It is important to choose a talk format that complements the purpose you set for talk. Talk formats are student participation structures that guide student talk by clarifying grouping interactions. Talk formats help you set the stage for science discussions. Different talk formats serve different purposes and provide different ways for students to practice the skills needed to engage in productive talk. Partner, small-group, and whole-group discussions are talk formats that provide three different ways to group students to engage in productive conversations.

Partner Talk	Small Group	Whole Group
Two students	Three to four students	Whole class

HOW DO I PLAN FOR PARTNER TALK?

Talking with a partner provides students an opportunity

- to actively listen to another student's idea,
- to make sense of ideas (either their own or the ideas of others) that may not be fully formed before going public,
- to practice sharing their reasoning with evidence as an informal introduction to the science practice of arguing from evidence (see Practices p. 48).

In partner talk you pause; give students two or three minutes to individually consider a question, comment, or observation; and then give them time to discuss it with a partner. Planned partner talk may be used to elicit prior knowledge, share observations, and clarify or expand thinking. It can also be employed in the spur of the moment when something puzzling or unexpected happens. Taking a pause to individually think and share thoughts with a partner can offer the group different perspectives and spark new conversations about the puzzling moment.

Tip *Provide students with a few minutes to write down their thoughts before beginning the discussion with a partner*

Often we are excited and ready to jump into conversations without providing ourselves time to consider what we want to share or how we want to phrase that information. An important part of scaffolding talk for students in any format is silent individual thinking time before entering into a conversation.

Access and Equity

For any engagement in a talk format, you need to consider whether students need shared knowledge or information to participate. Most equitable talk formats require students to have read, listened to, viewed, or manipulated something as a prerequisite for engaging in the talk.

Answers to Your Biggest Questions About Teaching Secondary Science

The following organizer can help to slow the process down to support thinking and provide a place to capture the ideas students want to share during partner talk.

Structured Partner Talk	
Think: My thoughts or understanding at this time	**Pair:** What I understand about what my partner is telling me
Share: Our common understanding after talking, what we want to share with others, or what we think is most important	

HOW DO I PLAN FOR SMALL-GROUP TALK?

We often cluster students to discuss a reading, plan and carry out an investigation, analyze data, or develop and work with models. The key to fostering productive small-group discussions around these tasks is for the task itself to be worthy of a group's interaction and engagement. Group-worthy tasks have features that inspire and demand conversations from students because the task cannot be completed well individually, without the support of others in the group. (For more on how to group students, see Chapter 2.)

Group-worthy tasks (see Figure 4.5) have the following features:

- Task has clear criteria for evaluating group and individual products.
  - Students know the timeline and product of the task.
- Task is open ended, productively uncertain, and requires complex problem-solving.
  - Students have an opportunity to offer multiple ideas or solutions and support the debate of ideas with evidence and rationales.
- Task provides multiple opportunities to demonstrate intellectual competence.
  - Students have the opportunity at multiple points in the task to offer ideas with tools, etc.
- Task is based on standards and addresses discipline-based, intellectually important content.
  - The conversation is content worthy and advances student sense-making about the ideas that are the target of your instruction.
- Task requires positive interdependence and individual accountability.
  - The task cannot be accomplished without the communication of group members.

Figure 4.5 Features of group-worthy tasks

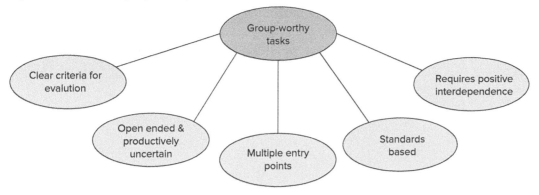

Tip 1 Assign student roles; assigning group roles provides students with a starting point and clear directions for accountability to each other and the group as a whole

Roles "activate" the opportunity to talk.

Student roles can range from logistical support of the task to deeper intellectual checkpoints in the conversation. Below are a few suggestions for roles in small-group work. We are not suggesting these are the only roles, nor that they are the only opportunity to enact talk.

Great Resources

To learn more about group-worthy tasks, read *Strength in Numbers: Collaborative Learning in Secondary Mathematics* by Ilana Horn.

Role	Purpose
Resource manager	• Sets up materials for the team • Makes sure everyone is touching materials according to rules
Recorder/reporter	• Calls the teacher over for team questions • Lets the teacher know when the group is ready for a check-in
Clarifier/facilitator • *Do we know what the word _____ means?* • *Can you say more about that?* • *Can you rephrase what _____ said?*	• Encourages clear communication • Monitors everyone's comprehension of science ideas
Questioner • *So what I think you are saying is ___. Is that right?* • *How do we know that?* • *What would happen if we changed _____?*	• Asks probing questions during the activity • Listens to questions posed by others and revoices
Skeptic • *Why do we think _____?*	• Probes for weakness in the product being developed
Progress monitor • *What have we accomplished so far?* • *What do we still need to know/do?* • *What can we add to _____?*	• Asks others to periodically measure progress towards goal
Floor manager • *Can we take a minute to hear from _____?* • *Who has not had a chance to weigh in on this?*	• Monitors the airtime of individuals in the group with the goal of ensuring everyone gets a chance to make ideas public

Tip 2 When beginning to introduce roles, start with just a few

Assigning all the roles is not the goal. The goal is to start with a few roles that are in alignment with the purpose set for the talk.

Tip 3 It is okay for two students in the group to have the same role

Tip 4 Use specific role cards with sentence starters on the desk or taped to the wall so they are visible and accessible to all students

Tip 5 Call out a role at different times during the task

This is one way to cue students to remember their roles. You can say things like, "It's time to hear from the floor manager!"

HOW DO I PLAN FOR THE WHOLE-GROUP TALK?

In whole-group discussions, everyone benefits from public access to the thinking of the entire group. During whole-group discussions, the teacher is both participant and facilitator. This takes practice! The goal of whole-group instruction is to promote peer-to-peer talk rather than student-to-teacher talk. Peer-to-peer talk provides students with the opportunity to support knowledge building in a public way as they reason with the ideas of others. Establishing and maintaining norms for a safe environment to offer and critique ideas publicly is instrumental to the success of whole-group discussions. Here are four ways to provide the whole class with access to each other's thinking:

1   Ask students to add to a peer's comment.
2   Ask students for evidence or reasoning behind their claims.
3   Ask students for clarification.
4   Ask students to share their different perspectives or understandings of the idea.

Access and Equity

If there is a dominant home language other than English in the classroom, be sure to learn some important phrases. Learn to count from one to ten and memorize words used for basic directions and common questions.

Tip 1 Provide visible sentence starters for students to practice with

We encourage you to make posters and ask students to contribute their own sentence starters about what to say when asking a question, respectfully disagreeing, or adding to the conversation.

Asking Questions	Respectfully Disagreeing	Adding to an Idea
• What made you think that? • What do you mean . . . ? • Can you be more specific about . . . ? • Why do you think that's important?	• I disagree with the idea because . . . • I understand it differently. • I know where you are coming from, but I have a different idea.	I agree with you, and I also think . . . I agree with your idea, but couldn't you add . . . ?

Tip 2 What you model and affirm, students will pick up on

When you model using sentence starters it brings familiarity to a talk format that may not come naturally to your students.

Getting my students to start to talk was a struggle. I now have conversation cards and sentence stems taped to their desks for a look whenever they need it.

–HIGH SCHOOL CHEMISTRY TEACHER

DISCUSSION

How Do I Facilitate Different Types of Conversations?

Productive discussions do not happen by chance. Facilitators of classroom discourse help students do the following:

- clarify ideas,
- focus and build on the ideas of others,
- share their reasoning with others.

Facilitators of classroom discourse also offer important what-if questions to spark student thinking.

Facilitators and students alike will need guidance and practice to engage in productive classroom discourse. Students may struggle because they are unaccustomed to sharing their ideas with each other or listening carefully as a peer explains their thinking. We often ask students to share their thinking when it is in draft form and unclear to themselves. This causes them to sound stilted, and the discourse is full of stops and starts and punctuated with a lot of "I don't know." Because of this, students may be reticent to share their thinking with others. Facilitators may struggle because this type of talk is unpredictable and requires real-time improvisational skills.

Once you have anticipated what students might say or do (see Discourse p. 114), you will want to devise a plan for selecting the strategies for talking that support you in sequencing and connecting the ideas students are building.

Research has shown that developing a repertoire of talk moves helps teachers to orchestrate and support student discussions (Michaels & O'Connor, 2012). Talk moves are phrases you might use within a conversation to facilitate discussions. Different talk moves serve different purposes. In Figure 4.6 we share five categories of talk moves.

Figure 4.6 Talk moves

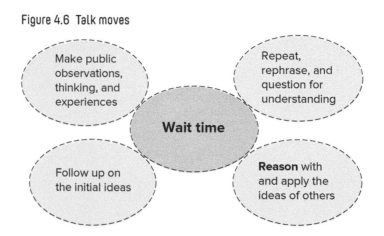

Struggling with wait time felt so awkward. I wanted to jump in to fill the void or rephrase my question, which usually lowered the cognitive demand of the question. I resorted to questions that only made space for yes/no answers. Now I actually put my hands behind my back and make myself count to ten on my fingers.

—NINTH-GRADE EARTH SCIENCE TEACHER

WHAT TALK MOVES DO I MAKE AND WHEN?

- **Wait time.** It may seem odd to have wait time featured as the first talk move. And as you see in Figure 4.6, wait time is depicted as central to the talk moves we share. As we stated previously, students need time to think before sharing. Not everyone can respond on the spot, nor should we expect that of our students. If we are to value and expect sense-making in the classroom, we must provide time for students to examine their own thinking. Pausing gives everyone the opportunity to prepare what they would like to say and how they want to voice their ideas. One way to make conversations more equitable is to pay close attention to your wait time. Wait time is something that you have control over, and it can be used to support more thoughtful contributions from all of your students.

- **Making public observations, thinking, and experiences.** This category brings prior experiences and initial ideas into the conversation. It is here that you think about what ideas you want to surface for students and how to connect those ideas together to build understanding. Some prompts that could be useful in making those connections apparent are:
  - What do you notice?
  - What do you think is happening here?
  - What experiences have you had that might be similar?

Tip 1 Record these observations in a public way so they are verbally and visually represented to the class

- **Repeat, rephrase, and question for understanding.** This category is about making sure everyone has heard the idea and is clear about its meaning. This is not about evaluating the merit or correctness of the idea. Instead, it is to help you and your students hear and understand the idea that was made public. Asking for rephrasing is a way to ensure others in the class have a clear understanding of what was said, even if the idea is incorrect. By doing this you are setting the stage for students to listen to each other's ideas and opening up the opportunity for student cross talk. Some useful prompts are:
  - Who can repeat what _____ said in their own words?
  - Can you rephrase what _____ said in your own words and check with them to see if that was what they meant?

Tip 2 Ask students to repeat or rephrase each other's ideas

By doing this you are signaling that students' ideas have value and that you care what they think. Further, when students revoice their peer's ideas, it shows they have listened to each other's ideas, not just the teacher's. Caution: Be careful when you rephrase students' ideas to not overwrite their ideas with your own.

One of the hallmarks of traditional schooling is a sense of urgency. This leads to students teeming to be first in response and being rewarded for being the quickest speaker during a lesson. Unlearning this tendency as an educator and encouraging and reinforcing wait time with students is one way to elevate reasoning over speed. This results in a more equitable learning environment because all students have a chance to develop and share their reasoning.

DISCUSSION

Identity & Access

Encourage students to use the name of the student whose ideas they are revoicing. For example, "I think Odelis's idea about energy is ... ." This ensures that the original speaker gets credit for their contributions and keeps students from feeling like others are receiving credit for their ideas.

Tip 3 **Do not use rephrasing as a management tool to catch someone who is not listening**

The purpose of these strategies is to invite student participation, not to penalize students for off-task behavior. Classroom norms and agreements are what students and teachers can lean on to encourage student engagement during classroom discussions (see Norms p. 71). When students experience classroom discussions as an authentic exchange of ideas, they may be more willing to engage in them.

Tip 4 **Rephrasing gives you an opportunity to connect words or language to science**

Tip 5 **Small groups are a good place to try out this strategy before using it for whole-group discussions**

- **Follow up on the initial ideas.** There are times when you and your class need to know more about what a student is saying beyond what a simple rephrasing might supply. In this case, you are signaling to the students that you genuinely are interested in what they are saying and you and the class want to know more. Useful prompts might be:
  - Can you tell me more about that?
  - Can you give an example of that?
  - What do you mean when you say_____?

Tip 6 **Follow-ups are particularly useful when a student's comment seems off topic or confusing**

This gives the student time to share more of their thinking and you more of an opportunity to see the connections the student is making.

- **Reason with and apply the ideas of others.** There are times when you will need to support students in reasoning further with an idea they offered or an idea another student shared. That may require asking for more information from the individual student or the whole group. This information may be needed to push student thinking in the following ways:
  - Ask for evidence or explanations:
    - What made you think that?
    - How did you arrive at that conclusion?
  - Ask for alternatives or what-if questions:
    - Does anyone have an alternative idea?
    - What might make the outcome different?
    - What if we . . . ?
  - Ask for consistency:
    - What do these observations have in common?
    - Where have we seen this before?
  - Ask someone to add to an idea:
    - Who can add on to that idea?
    - Can anyone take that suggestion further?

Tip 7 *It is important to think about the sequencing of ideas and how they connect to each other so that you can use these talk moves in combination with one another to serve your purpose for the discussion of ideas*

Using these talk moves can greatly impact students' engagement with science content and the SEPs. When you begin to use talk moves, especially with students learning to participate in discourse during lessons, you may experience resistance. Consistent usage of talk moves can help to move your classroom from one where students only listen to one where they talk to participate in the learning process. That is where classroom norms (see Norms p. 71) and repetition can support you in developing the kind of community you want in your classroom.

Great Resources

For more about how to sequence talk moves, read *Ambitious Science Teaching* by Mark Windschitl, Jessica Thompson, and Melissa Braaten.

DISCUSSION

How Do I Monitor Classroom Talk?

After you have planned for classroom discourse, selected a talk format, and thought about which talk moves you will try out, it is time to start thinking about how you will monitor students' conversations. How will you know that the conversation is supporting students in reaching the learning goal that is the target of your instruction? A big part of monitoring student conversations is anticipating. This involves thinking about what students might say and the strategies they will use. As you think about anticipating, consider the following strategies:

- Consult other colleagues and look at resources to gain a broader view of what students might say and do.
- Include both correct ideas and divergent ideas in your monitoring tool.
- Include questions you think students might ask.
- Think about connections among the ideas you want students to discuss and how you might respond to those ideas (see Facilitation, p. 124).

Tip Use the sentence stems you give students to help you think about their possible questions and responses (see Discourse p. 114).

Teaching in Flexible Settings

In a hybrid or virtual setting, using a virtual monitoring document will help you keep track of student responses and can serve as a form of classroom data.

WHAT MIGHT I RECORD AND WHY?

There are many ways to keep track of what students are saying and doing as they engage in tasks. These strategies range from writing notes for yourself on a blank sheet of paper to a preplanned monitoring tool complete with anticipated student ideas and questions filled out ahead of time. Because you have so many things to attend to during a classroom period, a preplanned monitoring tool will help you keep track of each group's progress. This will aid you in on-the-spot thinking so that you can decide what you want students to share publicly with the whole class to support learning.

Here is a sample monitoring chart of student conversations from the seabird readings.

Groups	Ideas to Listen For				Questions to Keep Track Of
	Feeding The birds are fast flyers and dive for prey of small schooling fish. Recently it is increasingly common to eat pipefish, which has less nutritional value, because previous prey is less available.	**Before eggs hatch** Courtship rituals include bowing and preening. Murres are monogamous and pairs split if unsuccessful. They nest in large colonies in close proximity. A single egg is incubated on the bare rock of the cliff face. Egg shape may influence the transfer of heat during incubation. Both parents take shifts in incubating the egg. Eggs are specific colors and patterns for recognition. If eggs are lost, females will lay a second egg that is usually less viable. Murres molt (lose feathers right after breeding) and are then flightless for one to two months.	**After eggs hatch** After hatching of egg parents take shifts in feeding hatchling. When food is low and foraging takes a long time, unattended chicks often die due to predation.	**Migration and movement** Murres spend most of their time at sea and only come to land to breed. They spend the winter far from breeding grounds. Adults return to the same colony and location to breed.	What do the prey of the murre eat? Why is their normal prey less available? What are the predators of the murre? What does the shape of the egg have to do with viability?
Group 1					
Group 2	Change in food				
Group 3		How do they get food if they are flightless?			
Group 4					
Group 5					
Group 6					
Group 7			What eats the chicks?		
Group 8					

Teacher moves

Group 2: Push to clarify thinking about why birds switched to a different food source.

Group 7: Needed to redirect thinking about nesting and available food sources. The whole class needs to hear this.

Unexpected student contributions

I wonder if there was a temperature change.

HOW DO I KNOW WHAT MY STUDENTS KNOW, AND HOW CAN I USE THAT INFORMATION TO PLAN AND MOVE THEM FORWARD?

After building a positive science community, organizing your class, engaging students in doing science, and helping them see the value in talking about science, it is important to find out what your students know and what they can do. Your students will show their understanding in many ways, including written, verbally, and visually. You will gather data on their thinking and give them feedback to help support them in engaging in science. As you do this, you will better understand what they can do and adjust your practice to take their ideas into account.

This chapter will help you understand how to assess students in science and help you in planning to meet your students' needs. We will discuss how to uncover student ideas at the beginning of a unit and how to design and evaluate a summative assessment task. Since you will not want to wait until the end of a unit to find out what your students know and are able to do, you will want to include formative assessments. This happens when you ask students to share their understanding and ideas in various ways at different times within a lesson sequence or unit. You can evaluate what they know and can do and then modify your instruction based on their responses. Providing feedback to students helps them gauge their progress in moving toward the goals of the lesson or unit, showing them how close or far they are. The aim is to improve student performance and understanding.

Classroom data are bits of information or artifacts that teachers can access and use to learn about their own teaching practice or that of others. Collecting and analyzing this data from your classroom should happen frequently. We discuss the use of student notes to help them understand the importance of documenting ideas to build understanding of the world. Giving students many opportunities to show their expertise in your class and share their understanding of science ideas, practices, or concepts is essential since they can apply what they know and can do to novel situations to solve a problem.

This chapter answers questions about how to determine what your students know and can do and how you can use that information to move forward. It answers the following questions:

- [ ] **How do I plan for assessing student learning?**
- [ ] **How do I use information from formative and summative assessments?**
- [ ] **How do I analyze classroom data?**
- [ ] **How do I support student learning with feedback?**
- [ ] **What is the role of student notes?**
- [ ] **How can I give students multiple opportunities to show they have expertise in a concept?**

As you read about these topics, we encourage you to reflect on the following questions:

- [ ] **What does this mean to me?**
- [ ] **What else do I need to know about this?**
- [ ] **What will I do next?**

How Do I Plan for Assessing Student Learning?

Assessment in a science class can take many forms. In this section we will focus on how to uncover student ideas at the beginning of a unit and how to design and evaluate a summative assessment task. (For strategies on assessing learning either at the end of a unit or during a lessons cycle, see Formative and Summative Assessments p. 136.)

A *pretest* or *probe* is one way to find out what students know before you start a unit. This kind of assessment can help you identify students' alternative conceptions that are not supported by scientific evidence. Then you can provide opportunities for students to reason about ideas that are currently scientifically accepted. One way to do this is to share a phenomenon related to the learning goal and ask students to explain how it happens. Their responses will help you plan instruction. You may decide to include evidence for students to help them reason about the phenomenon in ways that support them in aligning their ideas with those that are accepted by scientists.

The goal of a summative assessment is to evaluate student learning at the end of a group of lessons or an instructional unit. It is often focused on a specific standard or benchmark. A summative assessment can take the form of what we commonly think of as a written test or quiz, but it could also be a project or oral presentation. In science, summative assessments should have students doing science by engaging in the Science and Engineering Practices. These assessments should also support students in connecting new and prior knowledge rather than just assessing students' ability to recall knowledge about what scientists have already found out. Before you design an assessment task, you need to *define what you want students to know and be able to do.* This should be done before starting a unit. Take a look at the standards for your state or district to see what to address in your classroom. Here are some tips for designing assessments.

Great Resources

Formative assessment probes can be used to elicit student ideas. The *Uncovering Student Ideas* series of books by Page Keeley (see https://bit.ly/3jCrduY) offers probes for different disciplines and grade levels.

Tip 1 Make sure that the goals for the unit and the task are grade-level and subject appropriate

Check out the Next Generation Science Standards (NGSS) progressions for the Disciplinary Core Ideas (DCIs), Science and Engineering Practices (SEPs), and Crosscutting Concepts (CCCs) to see what is grade-level and subject appropriate.

Great Resources

- An example for the practice of constructing explanations and designing solutions, https://ngss.nsta.org/Practices.aspx?id=6
- Disciplinary Core Idea progressions, https://bit.ly/3Jua3L4
- Science and Engineering Practices progressions, https://bit.ly/3jbfm7F
- Crosscutting Concepts progressions, https://bit.ly/3WKfmsN

Tip 2 Choose a task that aligns with your learning goals and what you will be doing in the classroom

This will help you gather information about how well students understand the learning target (see Lesson Planning p. 60).

Tip 3 Analyze the questions or prompts on your assessment to make sure they evaluate students' knowledge of the big ideas in science and not just obscure facts that require memorization

> With three-dimensional learning, science students will need to explain their understanding when being assessed. Picking a "right answer" from a list won't show that they have done any science practices or connected their new knowledge with previous knowledge to solve a problem.
>
> —STANDARDS SPECIALIST

WHAT DO I INCLUDE IN A SCIENCE ASSESSMENT TASK?

Access and Equity

Consider having tasks that have low floors, high ceilings, and wide walls. These are tasks that provide a way for all students to get started (low floor) but have different ways that students can engage in the task, some of which are more sophisticated than others (high ceiling). There may not be one single path to complete the task, so students can explore multiple ways to get to an answer (wide walls).

A phenomenon should lead the task.	• This is an observable event that occurs in the universe. We can use science to explain or predict it. • It makes the task understandable and coherent for students. • Have the phenomenon be relevant to students as well as engaging.
Reasoning with both science ideas and science practices, tying them together with a crosscutting concept	• This helps students explain the phenomenon. • Students need to be explaining or solving a problem using at least one science practice as they complete the task and not just memorizing science facts. • They also need to use the DCIs involved to explain the phenomenon or solve the problem and tie the ideas together with CCCs. • You may choose to have a design challenge that uses science DCIs and engineering practices to solve it.
Application of ideas	• Include not only the ideas themselves but also their application in the task. • Students should be able to use the DCIs that were part of the goal of the unit to explain a novel situation.

Here is an example of how this could be done.

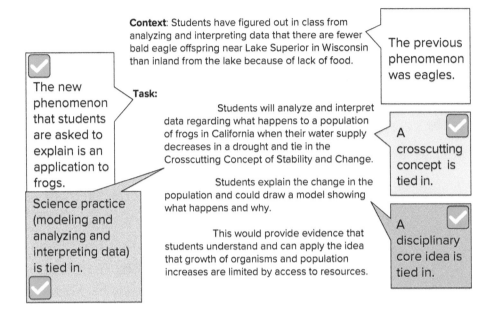

Context: Students have figured out in class from analyzing and interpreting data that there are fewer bald eagle offspring near Lake Superior in Wisconsin than inland from the lake because of lack of food.

The previous phenomenon was eagles.

The new phenomenon that students are asked to explain is an application to frogs.

Task:

Students will analyze and interpret data regarding what happens to a population of frogs in California when their water supply decreases in a drought and tie in the Crosscutting Concept of Stability and Change.

Students explain the change in the population and could draw a model showing what happens and why.

This would provide evidence that students understand and can apply the idea that growth of organisms and population increases are limited by access to resources.

A crosscutting concept is tied in.

A disciplinary core idea is tied in.

Science practice (modeling and analyzing and interpreting data) is tied in.

Great Resources

- Achieve's Science Task Prescreen at https://bit.ly/3iKHQkF can help you decide whether an assessment task is aligned to three-dimensional standards. The prescreener points out red flags that are common challenges found in science assessment tasks.

- If no red flags are found with the Science Task Prescreen, you may want to use Achieve's Science Task Screener at https://bit.ly/3YUtnGu. It is more in depth and assumes a deep understanding of three-dimensional learning.

- Steps to Designing Three-Dimensional Assessments That Connect to Students Interests, Experiences, and Identities, https://bit.ly/3jwSXS3

- An example of an evaluation of a summative transfer task along with a link to the task itself, https://bit.ly/3hTp2CT

- Integrating Science Practices Into Assessment Tasks, STEM Teaching Tool #30, https://bit.ly/3NLJW4d

- Prompts for Integrating Crosscutting Concepts Into Assessment and Instruction, STEM Teaching Tool #41, https://bit.ly/46glcZ1

HOW DO I PREPARE FOR AN ASSESSMENT?

Scoring will be based on how your school has decided to communicate student progress. It could be a percentage or a letter grade, or it could be a standards-based assessment such as *beginning, developing, sufficient*, or *advanced*. You will need to understand this before you develop a rubric.

1	**Anticipate and construct a student explanation or model of the phenomenon or a solution to the design challenge.**
	• Do this before giving the task to students.
	• This helps you focus on what you expect students to write or communicate.
	• Consider having students share their answers in other ways, such as orally or through drawings or graphs. (See Discourse p. 114 for more on anticipation.)
2	**Develop a scoring guide or rubric.**
	• Base this on what you want students to include in the explanation, model, or solution.
	• It could include "must haves"—what you need to have students include in their correct answer.
	• View the two scoring guides below specific to explanations and modeling.

Scoring guide for writing a scientific explanation	Scoring guide for constructing a model
The "must haves" for a scientific explanation could be	For a model to explain the phenomenon, you may require
• a particular claim,	• certain parts of the model be present,
• a certain amount and type of evidence (e.g., three supporting data pieces or facts),	• the model represent or describe certain things.
• a certain science principle to tie together the claim and the evidence.	These categories can be scored as *missing*, *developing*, or *mastered*.

HOW OFTEN SHOULD I ASSESS STUDENTS?

Make formative assessment continuous as you observe students discuss, write, gesture, and draw their thinking about science ideas. Formal assessment, often called summative assessment, may happen every two weeks or as the class finishes a lesson set in which students have answered a broad question in science. Assessment can be cumulative as you progress through a unit and build on the assessment tasks that students have previously completed.

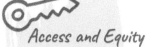

Access and Equity

Reading the assessment question aloud to students can help those who might struggle with reading. They may know the answer but struggle with reading the question.

You may also want to consider different options for how students convey their understanding to you. Some could write their responses, others could draw, and some could talk to you verbally or record their responses for you to watch later. For projects, it could be a combination of all of these methods in a multimedia format.

How Do I Use Information From Formative and Summative Assessments?

Assessments are important in a classroom so that teachers, students, and other stakeholders can see if students are meeting the goals of a lesson or unit. If there are students who are having difficulty reaching the learning target, they may need more help and the teacher may need to adjust instruction. Frequent formative assessment during a lesson can help teachers know whether students are making progress in understanding.

Summative assessment can inform teachers if students are able to synthesize the ideas that they have learned and are able to complete a task related to what they have been doing in class. In class, summative assessments are those that come at the end of a lesson set or a unit. (See Assess Learning p. 132 for information on designing summative assessments.) Results from these tests can instruct teachers on what students know and can do. Analyzing the results can inform future instruction since science builds on previous knowledge and understanding. If students do not do well on a summative assessment, it might mean that you need to figure out a way to circle back and reteach a concept in a different way.

It is important that assessment results measure student understanding and not compliance with format or other aspects that do not relate to what students understand and are able to do. For example, do not take off points for a student forgetting to write their name on the paper, stapling pages differently than how you direct them to, or writing in a color other than black. You may devise other ways to deal with these types of issues rather than giving students a lower score.

Other summative assessments could come from the state or national level. State testing for science provides the district and the public with a snapshot of students' progress with understanding and being able to carry out SEPs that are included in the state's science standards.

Formative assessment happens when you ask students to share their understanding and ideas in various ways at different times within a lesson sequence or unit. This allows you to evaluate what they know and can do at a certain point or points and then modify your instruction based on their responses. If you find out that many students do not understand a particular concept or have alternative conceptions about what a scientific model is, then you can bring in new ways to help students understand. Formative assessment can take many forms.

WHAT ARE SOME FORMS OF FORMATIVE ASSESSMENT?

We will share several types of formative assessment. Some ask for students' assessment of their own understanding, some ask for students to present their reasoning, and some ask for students to engage in a discussion with others about their understanding.

Ultimately, being able to quickly respond with feedback to student ideas can help them develop new ideas about science concepts and practices and how to connect the two. Feedback also acts as a diagnostic tool to help teachers see where they might need to provide students with other opportunities for understanding.

Type of Formative Assessment	How to Use It
Gestures	One quick way to assess student understanding is with a thumbs-up or thumbs-down. A teacher might show different models and have students give a thumbs-up for which one they think best explains a concept in science.
Discussion	Listen as students discuss their ideas in a whole-class setting as well as in groups. A teacher can then ask further questions, such as "Why do you think that?" and "What evidence do you have for your claim?" to help guide them to ideas that are supported by scientific evidence. Sentence stems can help them share their current understanding or questions. (See Talk Formats p. 120; Monitoring Discourse p. 128.)
"I used to think . . . , but now I think . . . "	Having students tell a teacher verbally or in text about what they used to think about a science idea and what they now think gives teachers insight into students' understanding at a particular time.
Whiteboards	If each student or group has an erasable whiteboard, a teacher can have them draw models, write short explanations, or show connections between ideas they've learned. The teacher can look around the room and see the range of understanding in the class.
Cartoons	Have students draw a simple cartoon explaining the science concept that is included in their learning target. The teacher can quickly see how students understand the concept and provide extra help for those who are missing essential components of the idea.
Fist to Five	Ask students to hold up zero to five fingers based on how much they understand a science idea. Zero would mean that they feel uncertain about their own understanding or are confused, and five means that they understand the concept well and can explain it to others. The teacher can then provide opportunities for students to work together to support collective understanding of the idea.
Think-Pair-Share	Give students time to think about a problem and then have them share with a partner. Students are more likely to share in a small group, so the teacher has an opportunity to move around the classroom listening to many responses. A large-group discussion can happen afterward with the teacher asking probing questions to help students who have difficulty in communicating their understanding or have questions, or to sequence ideas from the small groups to build class understanding.
Fishbowl	Five or six students are selected to be in the center (fishbowl) of a circle. They discuss and argue their ideas about a probe given by the teacher while the rest of the class listens and evaluates what the students in the fishbowl are saying. The roles can be switched so that all students get a turn. Students can record the ideas that surface during the discussion for a writing activity afterwards. The teacher can use what the students in the fishbowl say to guide further instruction.

(Continued)

ASSESSMENT

(Continued)

Type of Formative Assessment	How to Use It
Phenomenon probes	A familiar phenomenon is shown to students and different explanations for the phenomenon are listed. Include possible preconceptions and some explanations that are not supported by evidence as choices. The teacher can plan on addressing those ideas during the lesson or unit.
Gallery walk	Students post their model, explanation, or results of a project or investigation on whiteboards or poster paper around the room. Everyone in the class evaluates each of the products by putting sticky notes with their thoughts on the displays. This could include ideas about the parts that were included in the model or explanation as well as what they thought were strengths or things that could be improved upon.
Exit ticket	A short application of what was learned in the lesson is given to students to complete at the end of the class. A teacher can look at the responses and plan for the next day depending on how well students can answer the question. Another purpose for exit tickets can be to get information from students about their experience with the task. This will help in designing future tasks.

Great Resources

- *Science Formative Assessment* by Page Keeley offers 75 practical strategies for linking assessment, instruction, and learning (see https://bit.ly/4a36F4N). Each strategy has a description, an explanation of how it promotes student learning and informs instruction, and tips on how to design and administer it.

- Formative assessment probes can be used to elicit student ideas. The *Uncovering Student Ideas* series of books by Page Keeley (see https://bit.ly/3jCrduY) offers probes for different disciplines and grade levels.

Notes

How Do I Analyze Classroom Data?[1]

Classroom data are classroom information or artifacts that teachers can access and use to learn about their own or others' teaching practice. Usually, the term *data* is reserved to describe student-produced data such as classwork, homework, or assessment responses. This is an important component of classroom data that can shed light on what students understand at a specific moment in time but is limited in telling the whole story of the classroom. Seeking other sources of classroom data is important for better understanding of how what students encounter in the classroom impacts what they learn.

WHAT COUNTS AS CLASSROOM DATA?

There are three categories of data in a classroom. The figure below shares these categories and two examples of each.

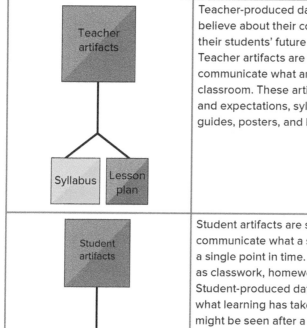

Teacher artifacts Syllabus, Lesson plan	Teacher-produced data often highlights what teachers believe about their content area (Stipek et al., 2001) and their students' future goals or careers (Sztajn, 2003). Teacher artifacts are teacher-produced documents that communicate what and how learning takes place in the classroom. These artifacts include things such as rules and expectations, syllabi, lesson and unit plans, pacing guides, posters, and books on display in the classroom.
Student artifacts Classwork, Assessment data	Student artifacts are student-produced documents that communicate what a student knows and understands at a single point in time. These artifacts include things such as classwork, homework, and assessment responses. Student-produced data show the teacher and students what learning has taken place. Student-produced data might be seen after a task has been solved or during the reasoning process on whiteboards or worksheets, or they might be shared verbally.

(Continued)

[1] This section is reprinted with permission from *Answers to Your Biggest Questions About Teaching Secondary Math,* by Frederick L. Dillon, Ayanna D. Perry, Andrea Cheng, and Jennifer Outzs. Thousand Oaks, CA: Corwin, 2022.

ASSESSMENT

(Continued)

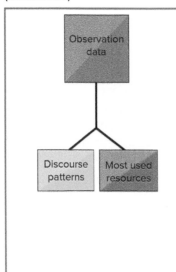

Observation data refers to anything that can be seen and includes who raises their hand first, how papers are returned to students, how students are commonly seated, and what information is written on the board. These data can clue visitors in to what the culture and norms of the classroom are. Observation data can support the teacher in learning how classroom norms and activities are taken up in the learning community. For example, if one of the classroom norms is that students ask questions of their elbow partners before talking with the teacher, an observer might record how many times students follow that norm compared to the number of times students ask the teacher first when they have questions. These data are easiest to collect with another set of eyes, whether they be a video camera or a colleague. It is difficult to manage the work of learning in the classroom and collect observation data simultaneously.

HOW DO I DECIDE WHAT DATA TO COLLECT?

Teachers should collect their data based on what they aim to learn about in their classroom.

Each form of data that exists in the classroom tells one part of the story of the classroom. For example, a teacher might be interested in learning who volunteers to share their thinking most often in class and what contributes to their comfort. To learn about this, a teacher could

- create a seating chart for the day and record tally marks based on the number of times a student raises their hand to share their thinking with the class,
- focus on one group during the lesson and record tally marks for the number of times different students in the group ask questions or share their thinking with other group members,
- give students a survey to ask them about how comfortable they are sharing their thinking in large- or small-group settings,
- focus on the volunteering tendencies of their highest or lowest achievers.

Each of these data points provides information about how comfortable students feel about sharing their thinking and the circumstances that make sharing easier.

HOW CAN I ANALYZE THE DATA I HAVE COLLECTED?

Once you have decided on what you want to learn, you need to develop a plan for data analysis. You can follow these tips to support you in using the data you have collected.

Tip 1 | Make sure you have just enough data

One of the biggest misconceptions about data analysis in a classroom is that you have to analyze all of the data you have access to in order to learn about your area of interest. This is not true and can result in you feeling overwhelmed. Instead, narrow your scope so that you are looking at enough data to support you in learning about your practice. For example, if you are wondering what your students understand of a recently taught topic, you can select a range of student work to analyze. This might be reading through half of the exit tickets at random or purposefully selecting a set of students' work, including some work that was successfully completed, some that was partially completed, and some in which students demonstrated significant struggle (Blythe et al., 2015).

Tip 2 Find some teachers to analyze your data with you

You will learn more and more deeply if you share your classroom data with others. Teachers outside of your classroom may see things in your data that you don't notice. These larger noticings can help you improve your practice in ways that you may not have initially considered (Blythe et al., 2015).

Tip 3 Use a protocol to make sure the conversation stays on track

Structured conversations about classroom data may seem constricting, but it can be scary to share your classroom data with others. Protocols are tools that teachers can use to narrow data discussions and keep the conversations focused on what you want students to learn.

> **Great Resources**
>
> Visit https://www.schoolreforminitiative.org/protocols/ to see a list of protocols. Some notable ones to get you started are Describing Students' Work, Atlas Looking at Data, and Change in Practice.

How Do I Support Student Learning With Feedback?

Once a teacher analyzes data to understand what students have learned, they will need to provide their students with feedback. It is one of the best ways to amplify learning. But what exactly *is* feedback? Simply put, it is information about how close or far a student is from reaching a stated goal. Feedback can be provided less as an evaluation and more with the aim of improving student performance and understanding (see Formative Assessment p. 136).

Here are some well-researched ideas about feedback (Stenger, 2014):

- Oral feedback is slightly more effective than written feedback.
- Feedback can be effective at all stages of learning ideas.
- Feedback can be effective coming from many different sources (teachers, peers, parents), but teacher feedback is the most effective.
- Students improve most when feedback is given about *both* mistakes *and* areas where the students do well. Both praise and redirection are warranted in effective feedback.

HOW DO I DISTINGUISH FEEDBACK FROM ADVICE?

Great Resources

The Educational Endowment Foundation provides information about feedback on its site at https://bit.ly/3ulgzZt

Grant Wiggins in *Understanding by Design* (2012) made a helpful distinction between feedback and advice. Advice is often unasked-for comments about how to do something better. Most teachers offer advice. Feedback, on the other hand, is information about how close or far from a goal the student has gotten. Here are two examples to illustrate the difference.

Feedback	Advice
"Your goal was to make your graphs neater and easier to understand than in your last lab report. However, the lack of units here makes this graph still difficult to understand."	"Put units on both axes."
"Your goal was to make sure all the givens in your problem set are listed and the correct equation to use is listed in symbolic form. In Problem 12, there seems to be a mismatch between your givens and your equation."	"Try a different equation for these givens."

This approach requires students to have a goal. We'll discuss goal setting in a bit.

You might notice that the feedback is longer, and if you are *writing* feedback, that can be difficult to accomplish with a full class of students. That said, because goals are set by students, the path of providing feedback helps students self-govern. Given how valuable feedback is for student learning, how do you offer it without making your job entirely about assessment and therefore undoable?

Take a look at these tips for more ideas about how to provide feedback.

Tip 1　Give verbal feedback in 1:1 meetings with students or as you circulate your room while students work

Ask that students write down the feedback you offer so that they do not forget what you tell them.

Tip 2　Allow students an opportunity to act upon the feedback

If all of your feedback is given on an assignment only after it is graded, there is no opportunity to revisit it. Most students will ignore your comments at that point and focus only on the grade.

Tip 3　To allow time for students to act upon your comments, give feedback mid-project

This is especially helpful as students write up the conclusions to the investigations, or if there is a work day for working on problem sets.

Tip 4　It is also okay to give advice

Advice is not bad, and it also provides direction for the students. Their goal might not align with all your expectations, so you still want to help students understand their performance versus the assignment requirements.

Students need clarity about the goal of feedback—to help them improve—so they should know what to do with the feedback they are given. Here are some actions following an assignment that allow for improvement.

Tip 1　Students may resubmit a larger piece of work, such as the conclusion to an investigation, addressing the feedback

This can be as complicated as a rewrite or as simple as annotations made by the student for each piece of written feedback received from the teacher.

Tip 2　The teacher may choose to interview a student about feedback given and what they might do differently or what they now know

HOW DO I GET STUDENTS TO SET GOALS?

Setting goals for students is often implicit; otherwise they may just adopt the goal of "do what the rubric tells me." That, however, might not yield great improvement from the student.

You may want to have students set SMART (**s**pecific, **m**easurable, **a**ttainable, **r**elevant, **t**imely) goals. Encouraging students to set their own goals helps them to feel a vested interest in those goals. The timeline of a goal can be a day, a unit, or a semester.

You may want to have students start a goal with "I will figure out . . . " or "I will make sense of . . . "

Here is an example of how a student's goal for explaining how a small seed grows into a large tree can be a SMART goal.

Phenomenon: A small seed grows into a large tree.	
Goal: "I want to figure out by the end of this unit how a seed can grow into a large tree. I will need to know what goes in and out of the tree and what happens inside the system of the tree."	
Specific	This is specific because it has the end point of being able to explain how a seed can grow into a large tree.
Measurable	Students can assess their progress by looking at what they have figured out and what they still need to figure out (for example, "I know what things go into the tree, but I'm not sure what is happening inside the tree and what goes out").
Attainable	The goal of explaining how a seed grows into a tree is attainable during a unit at different levels for both middle school and high school students. A storyline that lets them gather data step by step helps with this process.
Relevant	Most students are curious about how plants grow since their lives depend on plants. You could encourage them to use an example from their life, such as a plant they observe near their home or at school.
Timely	This is an example of a class-wide timeline, but timeframes can also be individual.

Students also benefit from writing down their goals and keeping them in a place that is easily accessible. Having them check regularly on how they are meeting their goals is important; it is also important to consult with them periodically. Students can also share goal progress with parents and discuss with peers. If students do not meet a goal, then you can work with the student to create a plan for meeting the goal.

Notes

Answers to Your Biggest Questions About Teaching Secondary Science

What Is the Role of Student Notes?

Writing down the ideas of science is central to its practice. While science teachers certainly use notes in traditional ways, they can also use notes to help students understand the importance of documenting ideas to build understanding of the world in ways that the students would not in other courses.

HOW DO I HELP MY STUDENTS TAKE HELPFUL NOTES?

In most cases, notes are for the student who is recording them. This means students should have agency to decide how to take notes and choose what strategies help them best interpret what they are learning (see Agency p. 23). As a secondary purpose, and to reinforce science as something that is shared, notes should communicate a person's understanding to others.

For these reasons, we can encourage our students to organize their notes around storylines, phenomena, SEPs, and CCCs—all of which can help students learn and remember the science they do.

WHAT ARE SOME TIPS REGARDING BEST PRACTICES FOR NOTE-TAKING?

Students can use notes

- as a reference to see the trajectory of their learning,
- to keep track of what they currently understand relating to a DCI, SEP, or CCC,
- to study for or take summative assessments,
- as a way to share evidence of their understanding with others.

Tip 1 *Students can draw on previous notes to construct a storyline about how their ideas have changed as they progressed through the lessons*

Encourage students to use written words and pictures to represent their ideas. Some useful prompts are:

- I used to think . . . , but now I think . . .
- What did we do? What question did we answer? What did we learn?

Tip 2 — Students can engage with data they have recorded beyond the initial experience and can use it to continue to make sense of a phenomenon

Teach students how to record data as a part of your classroom instruction so that students learn whether to include units, etc. They can keep track of patterns that they find in the data as a way to relate to the CCCs. They can also take notes about how they analyze and interpret data, which is an SEP.

Tip 3 — Students can keep track of evidence that will be used to answer a driving question that guides sense-making in a unit

This evidence that they encounter in a storyline can be used to construct an explanation, which is a scientific practice. See below for how developing and using a model, another scientific practice, can be the unifying idea for recording notes.

Tip 4 — Notes can be organized around Crosscutting Concepts

If students are trying to figure out carbon cycles in an ecosystem and how energy is involved, they can record in their notes what is included in the ecosystem and the inputs and outputs in the system. In another example, students might keep track of the effects of climate change when they are examining the cause of increased greenhouse gases in the atmosphere.

Tip 5 — Students who are adept at typing may prefer to take notes on an electronic device

These devices allow for applying emphasis (e.g., highlighting, bolding, color coding) more easily than handwritten notes might. You might also consider offering tablets that can be used with styli to allow for digital note-taking that can include making models through drawing. Livescribe pens, overlays, patty paper, wipeboards, and personal whiteboards are also tools that can support collective or individual note-taking. In addition, guided notes, printed notes, posted notes, and notes that contain visual components can aid students who are emergent multilinguals as well as any student who needs support in the course.

Tip 6 — Recording academic language and definitions in notes supports the development of shared language in class and ensures all students have access to the language of the discipline

Allow students to use their own words to write definitions to support them in reasoning about the concepts.

Tip 7 — Students can revisit problems solved in class to support them in completing problems at home

Students should record narrative along with the steps of problem-solving so that they can make sure they understand what they are doing.

WHAT ARE SOME GUIDELINES ABOUT HOW STUDENTS CAN TAKE NOTES?

Many instructors will want students to take notes on important ideas discussed in class. Here are some tips to make sure that process goes well:

- Studies circa 2014 (Mueller & Oppenheimer, 2014) indicated that handwritten notes were more effective than notes taken with a computer. However, replication efforts in 2020 (c.f. Morehead et al., 2019) have not shown a difference in factual recall, so multiple mediums can be used to take notes.
- Drawing/creating diagrams is rather difficult with a computer, and many science teachers put a premium on visual representation. The ease of drawing might push you toward handwritten notes.
- Be clear about what you want the students to write down. Some teachers create norms around it, such as, "If I write something on the board, then you write it also." Whatever the system, make sure that students know your expectations.
- Provide instruction on reducing sentences into phrases, diagrams, or any other shortcut. You can model this as you share ideas, and you can also borrow students' notes to share with the class for further modeling. Using students' notes from a previous term is often best. Note-taking is a skill that, once acquired, can support students in studying material when they are away from class.
- It can be helpful to divide notes into sections: one for the ideas themselves and one where students can interact with the notes by asking questions or writing down connections.
- You could give the students an image or diagram where the notes are the important words or processes that relate to that image or diagram.

In my virtual school teaching, I didn't give any notes. Students had everything at their fingertips. If I did, it was the terms and concepts in my words instead of their learning platform's jargon. I spent my time more on application of their "notes"/textbook.

—HIGH SCHOOL BIOLOGY TEACHER

Great Resources

Cornell notes and journaling are great systems for interactive note-taking:

Cornell notes, https://bit.ly/42TAhg7

"How to Create Authentic Writing Opportunities in the Science Classroom," by Hoa P. Nguyen, https://edut.to/3X11Nqw (Cornell journaling)

How to Use Science Journal for Kids in the Classroom— and Why, https://bit.ly/3oOULZF (Cornell journaling)

HOW CAN I USE NOTES TO HELP STUDENTS REFINE A MODEL?

Another way to organize notes focuses on developing and using models, as prescribed by using the SEPs. Encourage students to reinforce the notion that scientists write work down and continually refine their thinking by having students maintain a record of the models they create as they make sense of the world. Below is an example from a physics course where the teacher carefully reveals understanding about gravity and students are expected to refine their model as they figure out more.

On the first day of school, a physics teacher takes her students outside with a water balloon launcher and several water balloons. She knows that her students have an understanding of acceleration. Students launch balloons in four directions: 1) diagonally down, 2) horizontally, 3) straight up, and 4) at an upward angle, and the teacher encourages the students to launch each balloon to its maximum distance.

ASSESSMENT

The teacher then asks, "Once the water balloon left the launcher, how did the acceleration of each balloon compare?"

A student might respond with notes for the model like those in this table.

Observations	Model So Far
• Balloon 1 went to the ground quickly. • Balloon 2 went further than Balloon 1 and didn't seem to go toward the ground as fast. • Balloon 3 rose, then fell and splatted close to us! • Balloon 4 went so far.	• Balloon 1 had the greatest acceleration because it hit the ground the fastest. • Balloon 3 slowed on the way up (no acceleration), then fell, then sped up, and it went very fast by the time it hit the ground. So it had the second-greatest acceleration. • Balloon 2 had the slowest acceleration because it didn't have as much room to speed up like Balloons 3 and 4.

The teacher then informs the students, "Let's neglect air resistance. Assume that once they have left the launcher, all balloons have exactly the *same* acceleration. Please pull out your model notes and see if you can make any adjustments to your model and/or identify some next steps for your own research."

A student might respond with notes for the model like those seen here.

Observations	Model So Far
• Teacher states that all balloons, once they leave the launcher, have the same acceleration.	• Maybe I don't know all the details of *acceleration*. I thought it meant objects speed up. • But it appears as though acceleration isn't affected by direction, since all balloons went in different directions. • I'll look up *acceleration* in the textbook tonight.

After some reading and instruction on the mathematical definition of *acceleration*, including that an object accelerates in both speeding up and slowing down, the student might write something like this.

Observations	Model So Far
• According to my teacher *and* our textbook, acceleration includes both slowing down and speeding up. Also, an object can still be accelerating when it falls or turns.	• The balloon rising then falling was maybe accelerating the entire time? Could it have the same acceleration on the way up as it did on the way down?

Eventually, the student will be able to describe the model of acceleration due to gravity based upon other experiences, problems, and reading. Various rounds of note-taking to get to this determination might take several pages of a notebook.

Things to note in this scenario:

- Students' notes are directed toward making sense of both the actions of the balloon and of the teacher's statement about acceleration.
- Students will provide incorrect conclusions at various points and that is exactly as it should be. Models are always incomplete, and often incorrect, until more data is obtained. This helps reinforce the notion that science is about the refinement of ideas based upon data and analysis.
- Observations can be both observed actions of objects and new information obtained from either literature or the teacher.

How Can I Give Students Multiple Opportunities to Show They Have Expertise in a Concept?

At some point, exposure to an idea turns into expertise. When does this occur? First, there is the function of the amount of exposure. Advertisers typically use the "rule of seven," which states that a consumer needs to be exposed seven to eight times before they remember a brand name. This might guide your thinking about how many times a student should encounter a concept. Second, it is well established that spacing a concept over time yields better long-term recall (Kang, 2016). Those two ideas—frequency and spacing—are an excellent foundation for building student expertise.

WHEN ARE STUDENTS READY TO SHOW EXPERTISE?

The opportunities you offer to the students to engage with a scientific concept will help them understand both the theoretical and the practical nature of concepts. As an example, here are some ways that you might imagine exposing students to the idea of density, listed roughly in the order you might create the opportunities in your classroom.

General Action	How That Action Applies to Learning About Density	Likelihood of Student Expertise
Presenting a common phenomenon in science	"I have these two pieces of metal that are silver and shiny. Are they the same metal, or are they different? How might we tell?" Group may generate several ideas. If it doesn't come up, the teacher might say, "One way to test is to measure their densities. Let's explore this idea of density."	Unlikely
Initial lab exploration	Students are given a variety of objects and limited information about density. They might make hypotheses about which objects are most dense or least dense and justify their hypotheses.	Unlikely
Lecture	Teacher provides instruction about density, including its definition; example problems; and problem solutions.	Unlikely
Problem sets	Students are given structured problems to solve and then are provided feedback.	May have
Journals	Students need to write, using prose, answers to more complex problems. Sometimes journals might push thinking toward something such as volume by displacement: "How might you find the density of this group of 100 paper clips?"	May have

(Continued)

How Can I Give Students Multiple Opportunities to Show They Have Expertise in a Concept?

149

(Continued)

General Action	How That Action Applies to Learning About Density	Likelihood of Student Expertise
Class or small-group discussion	The same kinds of questions you offer in a journal can also be offered to groups in your class for discussion. Small-group discussion (versus whole-class discussion) usually yields a much higher percentage of the students speaking and thinking.	May have
Board work	This is often helpful after group discussion. Different groups might be encouraged to solve problems on the board about density. It is also often good for review of concepts for upcoming assessments.	May have
Lab	Students might find the identities of several oddly shaped pieces of metals by using density.	Likely
Review work	This can often take the form of competitive games in the class, highlighting students' understanding thus far.	Likely
Test or quiz	A physical or online summative assessment would have students engaging in problems similar to those in the problem sets. It would also ask conceptual questions about measurement (likely similar to the initial question) and questions from the lab.	Likely
Student presentations	Sometimes done in addition to or as an alternative to more traditional assessments, presentations are often good for assessing students' gestalt understanding of a concept. However, it is more difficult with presentations to discern students' detailed knowledge (such as problem-solving) of the concept.	Likely

The actions designated as those in which students *may have* expertise present both teachers and students opportunities for student choice about assessment of knowledge and skills. While engaging in these actions, a teacher might offer opportunities for students to take a short quiz—but the students choose *when*. This helps student agency by assessing them when they think they are ready and understand. The logistics of at-will quizzing are remarkably easier if the quizzing is done electronically so that the teacher can draw upon a variety of questions and shuffle those questions easily with a few clicks. The teacher might also offer short oral exams to each student as they engage in at-will quizzes over a period. These quizzes can be graded or not.

HOW DOES A SPIRAL CURRICULUM HELP IN CREATING OPPORTUNITIES?

A spiral curriculum involves the notion that students might visit an idea several times over the course of a year, or even several years, and in this progressive exposure to the concept, they gain expertise. By revisiting concepts in a more sophisticated way, students can build on ideas and become more proficient. This is a part of the NGSS

Teaching in Flexible Settings

If you are in a hybrid setting or have tech available, you can use resources such as Quizizz, Kahoot, Nearpod, Blooket, Quizlet Live, and Plickers to support your assessments.

where the learning progressions on each of the dimensions shows an increasing sophistication of student thinking (National Research Council, 2012). According to Jerome Bruner (1960), there are three crucial components of a spiral curriculum:

1   The student encounters an idea or concept multiple times, either over the course of a school year or over the course of their schooling.
2   Each time the concept is revisited, it is addressed in a more complex manner than before.
3   Each time the concept is revisited, it activates knowledge previously gained; there is a clear relationship between old and new learning.

Below is a model of how spiraling can happen in science education.

Spiraling can be particularly effective for teachers engaging in authentic projects in which they might need to revisit concepts in a variety of projects. It might also be a natural way that science is structured. In a physics course, for example, a student might visit the idea of gravity multiple times:

1   Initially, a teacher might ask students, "Do falling objects fall at a constant speed, or do they speed up, or do they slow down? Create an experiment to demonstrate your claim."
2   Next, a teacher might give students a mechanical timer and paper tape and encourage them to use those items to measure the acceleration due to gravity based upon a velocity versus time graph. This is more complex than just determining whether the object speeds up or not.
3   Eventually, a teacher might prompt students to calculate the acceleration due to gravity on the Earth's moon; on Mars; and on Europa, a moon of Jupiter. This requires a more complex understanding of the relationship between universal gravitation and the acceleration at the surface of a planet.

In each of these examples, the student is exploring gravity, going from the least complex idea to the most complex idea, and gaining expertise in what we mean when we use the term *gravity*.

ASSESSMENT

WHERE DO I GO FROM HERE? HOW DO I KEEP LEARNING AND GROWING?

As we begin the last chapter of this book, we reflect on the many components that make up effective teaching. It can feel overwhelming to be responsible for developing scientific reasoning and maintaining the safety and well-being of so many students. This book has sought to answer some of the most important questions teachers ask about these issues. Yet there is always more to learn. Our understanding of what we have shared with you has evolved over time through our teaching practice, and yours will likewise evolve for you as you gain experience and develop your expertise as a professional. Given our charge to increase the positive impacts we have on our students, we know that we must continue to move closer to great science teaching. We also know that your perception of great science teaching will shift as you engage in the profession. This teaching journey is worthy and rewarding. It allows you the honor and privilege of preparing your students for their futures and gives you the opportunity to inspire and make a difference in their lives.

This chapter reflects on your growth as an educator. Ask yourself:

- [ ] **What activities can I pursue to grow and learn?**
- [ ] **How do I advocate for myself and my students?**
- [ ] **What are some frequently asked questions from secondary science teachers?**

As you read about these topics, we encourage you to reflect on the following questions:

- [ ] **What does this mean to me?**
- [ ] **What else do I need to know about this?**
- [ ] **What will I do next?**

What Activities Can I Pursue to Learn and Grow?

As a beginning teacher you'll have many questions, and as you go you will learn a variety of things about the discipline you teach and about pedagogical strategies. You will learn to think about your content differently. You will begin to see connections within your discipline and across disciplines, and your students will help you to see core ideas differently just by the questions they ask. You will try out new procedures each year and adopt new ways to introduce, assess, and build on ideas.

It might seem overwhelming at first, but remember: No teacher knows or remembers everything no matter how long they have been in the profession. The important thing to know is that teaching is lifelong learning. Every time you have the opportunity to grow in your teaching, don't let it pass you by. The power of strengthening both your content knowledge and your teaching knowledge will make you a better teacher and model for your students. You can show students that learning is a lifelong endeavor.

WHERE DO I SEEK OUT PROFESSIONAL DEVELOPMENT?

There are many different resources you could draw from to support your ongoing professional development. Below are three options you might pursue.

1. **School-offered opportunities.** We recommend you first be aware of the professional development that your school and district put forward.

   - Within your school:
     - Attend professional development sessions led by in-school personnel.
     - Create a professional learning community with a group of colleagues.
     - Attend regular staff and department meetings.
   - Within your district:
     - Ask about in-district professional development sessions across schools.
     - Attend in-district offerings according to your interests and needs.

I dragged my feet to a district professional development about our new grading software and came away with connections to another biology teacher in my district who is exploring local phenomena in their classroom. We are now meeting to plan a lesson together. If I hadn't attended the grading PD, I would not have expanded my network.

—TENTH-GRADE BIOLOGY TEACHER

2 **Opportunities beyond your district.** Look for resources within your state and region.

- Look for conferences in your area, including in-person and virtual meetings. Remember, some options require preregistration and fees. Find out what your district will support you in registering for.
- Take courses and look for immersive science opportunities. Science is made up of many disciplines and there are always advances in content and technology being made. It takes work to keep up! If you are a teacher who is new to your specific discipline or who has transitioned to a grade or content area that is less familiar to you, taking courses can refresh your memory and help keep you up to date on current advancements in science and technology.
  - *Coursework.* The availability of flexible options, both online and in-person, makes taking courses more convenient and accessible. One advantage of your learning is that you gain a new perspective and you can re-experience what it is like to learn through a student lens. Also, remember that class fees and books are sometimes covered by scholarships, fellowships, or your district. Investigate if you can have your coursework partially or fully funded and whether you can earn continuing education credits (CEUs) for your coursework.
  - *Internships.* Many colleges and universities open up their laboratories for summer internships. This presents a great opportunity for you to experience the advancements your discipline is making with respect to doing science (see Practices p. 48). This also gives you an opportunity to experience the collaborative nature of the scientific process. Sharing these experiences with students helps them to see that we all are capable of doing science and contributes to the positive science identity in your classroom.
  - *Conferences.* It is important to also look for state and national conferences. Ask your colleagues about conferences that they recommend or were funded to attend. Many conferences have a theme or specialization for a particular purpose, so it pays to do some research to figure out the ones that best meet your needs. Think about ways you can share what you learn with colleagues at your school. You could ask in advance for time in a staff meeting to share resources or strategies you learned from attending the conference.
  - *Reading books about teaching.* Another way to engage in professional development is to read books about teaching, especially in the area of science. There are many excellent books included in the Great Resources sections of this book that will help you with your practice.

3 **Worldwide opportunities.** Look for opportunities outside of classrooms and lecture halls.

- There are many options to get into the field and learn about your discipline through the lens of research. Bringing back these authentic experiences to your classroom shows students that science exploration is not limited to the laboratory.

GROWTH

Great Resources

- Experience fieldwork with scientists to assess the diets of killer whales, https://bit.ly/3CFSvXU

- Learn about climate, plants, animals and systems in the Amazon, https://bit.ly/3CL7lMA

- Learn about biodiversity in the Galapagos, https://bit.ly/42ZR94S

WHAT PROFESSIONAL GROUPS CAN I JOIN OR START?

Teaching in isolation is hard to do. Just like our students, we benefit from the ideas that a diverse community can bring. Opening up our practice and listening to others helps us reflect on our understanding and be open to new strategies to improve our practice. There are many different groups you can join; some are formal organizations and some are groups you can initiate.

WHAT ARE SOME STATE OR REGIONAL ORGANIZATIONS I CAN JOIN?

Usually state or regional organizations have reasonable membership costs for preservice and in-service teachers. You can look for regional chapters among these organizations. Also, look at your state's education page for other opportunities and services. There are nationwide fellowships you can apply to. Fellowships combine both professional development and ongoing support throughout the school year from teachers outside of your school.

Great Resources

Explore these fellowship opportunities:

- Knowles Teaching Fellowship, https://bit.ly/42U7Oqy

- Hollyhock Fellowship, https://cset.stanford.edu/pd/hollyhock

Explore these associations:

- The National Association of Biology Teachers offers regional affiliations you can join. See a list of regional coordinators at https://bit.ly/449cg5C.

- The National Science Teaching Association offers a variety of opportunities to network with science teachers at https://www.nsta.org/#tab-network.

- PhysTEC offers fellowships and ways to learn with physics teachers nationwide. Learn more at https://phystec.org/join.

WHAT ARE SOME GROUPS I CAN INITIATE?

Teachers who collaborate with colleagues inside and outside of their schools are more effective (National Council of Teachers of Mathematics, 2014). A growing body of research shows that when teachers work more collaboratively, student outcomes can improve, teachers can be more satisfied in their jobs, and teacher turnover can decrease (Schleifer et al., 2017). When teachers collaborate, they benefit from sharing different expertise and hearing multiple perspectives. There are many possible reasons for initiating a collaborative teacher group and many topics a group might focus on. You may want to start a group to

- expand your vision of what good teaching and learning looks like,
- work together to develop tasks, projects, assessments, lessons, etc.,
- create a structure for observations of other teachers in your school,
- problem-solve together about different issues or topics,
- start a citizen science club at your school,
- create supportive relationships with colleagues who listen and care.

Starting a collaborative teacher group requires your group to attend to ideas that are relevant, to plan for facilitating professional learning, and to build trust among group members.

Great Resources

- Read about how a teacher started a critical friend group in Victor Chen's "Bringing a Slice of KSTF to My School: How Starting Critical Friends Groups Has Helped Create a Space for Professional Reflection and Discussion" at https://bit.ly/3pa27Hm.

- To learn more about how to maintain a collaborative teacher group, read "The Tale of a Successful Collaboration" by Mark Hartman, Heather Hotchkiss, and Kate Miller, https://bit.ly/3qTObl7.

- To learn more about starting an observation club, read Kylie Bertram's "Benefits of a Teacher Observation Group" at https://bit.ly/3CGCxN6.

Starting a book club is another way to discuss problems of practice with colleagues. Below is a list of some books aligned with the chapters of this text.

Chapter 1: How Do I Build a Positive Science Community?

- Archibald, G. (2016). *My life with cranes*. International Crane Foundation.
- Barres, B. (2018). *The autobiography of a transgender scientist*. MIT Press.
- Fausch, K. D. (2015). *For the love of rivers: A scientist's journey*. Oregon State University Press.
- Frank, A. (2018). *Light of the stars: Alien worlds and the fate of Earth*. W. W. Norton and Company.
- Harrington, J. N. (2019). *Buzzing with questions: The inquisitive mind of Charles Henry Turner*. Illustrated by T. Taylor III. Calkins Creek.

GROWTH

Jahren, H. (2016). *Lab girl*. Knopf.

Keating, J. (2017). *Shark lady: The true story of how Eugenie Clark became the ocean's most fearless scientist*. Illustrated by Marta Álvarez Miguéns. Sourcebooks, Inc.

Keller, E. F. (1984). *A feeling for the organism: The life and work of Barbara McClintock* (10th anniversary ed.). Macmillan.

Kimmerer, R. (2013). *Braiding sweetgrass: Indigenous wisdom, scientific knowledge and the teachings of plants*. Milkweed Editions.

Lanham, J. D. (2016). *The home place: Memoirs of a colored man's love affair with nature*. Milkweed Editions.

Love, B. L. (2019). *We want to do more than survive: Abolitionist teaching and the pursuit of educational freedom*. Beacon Press.

McGee, E. O. (2021). *Black, brown, bruised: How racialized STEM education stifles innovation*. Harvard Education Press.

Shetterly, M. L. (2016). *Hidden figures: The American Dream and the untold story of the Black women mathematicians who helped win the space race*. William Morrow.

Wilson, E. O. (2006). *Naturalist*. Island Press.

Chapter 2: How Do I Structure, Organize, and Manage My Science Classroom?

Almarode, J., Fisher, D., Frey, N., & Hattie, J. (2018). *Visible learning for science, grades K–12: What works best to optimize student learning*. Corwin.

Brown, B. A. (2021). *Science in the city: Culturally relevant STEM education*. Harvard Education Press.

Burant, T., Christensen, L., Walters, S., & Salas, K. D. (Eds.). (2010). *The new teacher book: Finding purpose, balance, and hope during your first years in the classroom*. Rethinking Schools.

Chapman, C., & Hyatt, C. H. (2011). *Critical conversations in co-teaching: A problem-solving approach*. Solution Tree Press.

Duncan, R. G., Krajcik, J. S., & Rivet, A. E. (Eds.). (2016). *Disciplinary core ideas: Reshaping teaching and learning*. NTSA.

Hammond, Z. (2014). *Culturally responsive teaching and the brain: Promoting authentic engagement and rigor among culturally and linguistically diverse students*. Corwin.

National Research Council. (2012). *A framework for K–12 science education: Practices, crosscutting concepts, and core ideas*. National Academies Press.

NGSS Lead States. (2013). *Next Generation Science Standards: For states, by states*. National Academies Press.

Nordine, J., & Lee, O. (Eds.). (2021). *Crosscutting concepts: Strengthening science and engineering learning*. NSTA.

Paris, D., & Alim, H. S. (Eds.). (2017). *Culturally sustaining pedagogies: Teaching and learning for justice in a changing world*. Teachers College Press.

Schwarz, C. V., Passmore, C., & Reiser, B. J. (2017). *Helping students make sense of the world using next generation science and engineering practices*. NSTA.

Chapter 3: How Do I Engage My Students in Science?

⬤ Ballenger, C. (2009). *Puzzling moments, teachable moments: Practicing teacher research in urban classrooms.* Teachers College Press.

⬤ Colburn, A. (2016). *Learning science by doing science: 10 classic investigations reimagined to teach kids how science really works, grades 3–8.* Corwin.

⬤ Fogler, H. S., LeBlanc, S. E., & Rizzo, B. R. (2008). *Strategies for creative problem solving* (pp. 52–53). Prentice Hall.

⬤ Green, J. (2020). *Powerful ideas of science and how to teach them.* Routledge.

⬤ Keeley, P., & Tugel, J. (2019). *Science curriculum topic study: Bridging the gap between three-dimensional standards, research, and practice.* Corwin.

⬤ National Research Council. (2012). Chapter 3: Dimension 1: Scientific and Engineering Practice. In *A framework for K–12 science education: Practices, crosscutting concepts, and core ideas.* National Academies Press.

Chapter 4: How Do I Help My Students Talk About Science?

⬤ Ballenger, C. (2009). *Puzzling moments, teachable moments: Practicing teacher research in urban classrooms.* Teachers College Press.

⬤ Brown, B. A. (2021). *Science in the city: Culturally relevant STEM education.* Harvard Education Press.

⬤ Cartier, J. L., Smith, M. S., Stein, M. K., & Ross, D. K. (2013). *5 practices for orchestrating productive task-based discussions in science.* National Council of Teachers of Mathematics.

⬤ Windschitl, M., Thompson, J., & Braaten, M. (2020). *Ambitious science teaching.* Harvard Education Press.

Chapter 5: How Do I Know What My Students Know and How Can I Use That Information to Plan and Move Them Forward?

⬤ Allen, D., & Blythe, T. (2004). *The facilitator's book of questions: Resources for looking together at student and teacher work.* Teachers College Press.

⬤ Blythe, T., Allen, D., & Powell, B. S. (2015). *Looking together at student work.* Teachers College Press.

⬤ Keeley, P. (2015). *Science formative assessment, volume 1: 75 practical strategies for linking assessment, instruction, and learning.* Corwin.

⬤ Keeley, P., & Eberle, F. (2005). *Uncovering student ideas in science: Another 25 formative assessment probes.* NSTA.

Chapter 6: Where Do I Go From Here? How Do I Keep Learning and Growing?

⬤ Keenan, H. (2021). Keep yourself alive: Welcoming the next generation of queer and trans educators. *Occasional Paper Series, 2021*(45), 12.

⬤ Kohli, R. (2021). *Teachers of color: Resisting racism and reclaiming education.* Harvard Education Press.

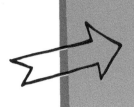

How Do I Advocate for Myself and My Students?

The education system can place a lot of demand both on you as a teacher and also on your students. Learning to advocate effectively for yourself and your students will play an important role in the sustainability of teaching and learning.

HOW DO I ADVOCATE FOR MYSELF?

- **Prioritize what matters to you.** Start by reflecting on what is most important to you with regard to your work. What are your goals for the year? How do you want to grow? Where do you get energized? Taking care of your physical needs as much as possible (sleep, eating lunch, using the restroom, etc.) are some examples of prioritizing yourself during the work day.

- **You are enough, just say no!** Our jobs ask a lot of us, whether from the system as a whole or from students, colleagues, families, and administration. It is okay and important to establish boundaries that feel healthy and sustainable to you. This may mean saying no to the picture of the perfect teacher that you aspire to be, to the extra responsibilities that keep you from excelling in your work as a teacher (especially beyond contract hours), or to classroom practices that hurt your students. This is much easier said than done, but it is important to return to your goals and determine how you are meeting or ignoring them.

- **Find allies.** Find and invest in fellow colleagues who uplift you. These are folks whose values might match your own. This means that you might need to walk around to chat with other staff, sometimes out of your own department. These allies can support you, give you advice, and overall help you feel a sense of belonging.

- **Cultivate joy for yourself.** Finding moments, people, places, or practices that bring your spirit joy are an important aspect of sustaining teaching. Cultivating joy and self-care can occur both in your professional life and your personal life. Professionally, this joy could come from your students, the activities you plan, giving students feedback, or more! Personal joy is specific to you.

- **Be an agent of change.** Seeing yourself as an agent of change is important in advocating for yourself and students. You can enact change, and you make a million decisions all the time! What are you in control of? What can you leverage in your context for change (allies, relationships, policies, systems, etc.)?

- **It is okay to change schools.** For a variety of reasons, you might be in a place where you are considering changing schools. If you feel like this is where you are and this is what you need to better advocate for yourself (and, more broadly, students in the education system at large), that is okay! You are allowed to change contexts!

Great Resources

Teachers of Color: Resisting Racism and Reclaiming Education by Rita Kohli; "Keep Yourself Alive: Welcoming the Next Generation of Queer and Trans Educators," by Harper Keenan, https://bit.ly/44gTnxK

HOW DO I ADVOCATE FOR MY STUDENTS?

- **Provide spaces for feedback.** Amplify students' voices in the classroom to help them make decisions that impact them. Let them choose how they want to learn or what they want to learn about. Let them evaluate how a specific activity or unit went. Give students space and time to reflect on how things are going in your classroom environment. Structure a discussion about how students are interpreting and enacting the classroom norms.

- **Collaborate and connect.** Sometimes you can advocate for students by getting them connections and resources that are beyond your scope. This could be professional opportunities for students, such as internships, career coaches, guest speakers, and conference opportunities. Or it could be a personal opportunity if you believe the guidance counselor, a behavioral specialist, or other professional might be better equipped to support that student. Conferencing with families is also an important part of advocating for students (see Communications p. 28).

- **Practice creative insubordination.** Education systems are complex. Sometimes to advocate for students we might need to go against a deficit school culture or a problematic practice or policy that is hurting our students. In these cases, finding ways to be "creatively insubordinate" can help you make progress (Gutiérrez, 2015). This could mean 1) protecting or providing opportunities that students deem important, such as extracurricular activities or student committees, 2) volunteering on building- or district-level committees and bringing in student perspectives, 3) using teaching practices in your classroom that affirm students, 4) sharing alternative strategies or pushing back against practices that hurt students, such as fast-pacing or high-stakes testing pressures, and/or 5) managing classroom and school behaviors in ways that affirm students, such as avoiding punitive disciplinary measures.

> As a teacher of color, I found out early in my career that the school system was so exhausting for me, more so than for my white colleagues. After reading about creative subordination, I have been able to rethink how I can sustain myself and work against this system that is hurting me and my students of color.
>
> **—EARLY-CAREER HIGH SCHOOL TEACHER**

- **Cultivate joy for your students.** Finding moments, people, places, or practices that bring joy to your students' spirits is an important aspect of building a positive classroom culture (see Community p. 10; Sense of Wonder p. 13).

GROWTH

Great Resources

- *Rethinking Sexism, Gender, and Sexuality*, edited by Annika Butler-Wall, Kim Cosier, Rachel Harper, Jeff Sapp, Jody Sokolower, and Melissa Bollow Tempel, https://bit.ly/445Qxf4

- *Teaching for Black Lives*, edited by Dyan Watson, Jesse Hagopian, and Wayne Au, https://bit.ly/431ggEh

- "Building Schools Where Students Are Free to Be Their Authentic Selves" by Stephanie García, https://bit.ly/44ijQez

- *Acting Out! Combating Homophobia Through Teacher Activism*, edited by Mollie V. Blackburn, Caroline T. Clark, Lauren M. Kenney, and Jill M. Smith

- *Stepping Up! Teachers Advocating for Sexual and Gender Diversity in Schools* by Mollie Blackburn, Caroline Clark, and Ryan Schey, https://amzn.to/3CGSgfd

- "Advocacy as a Practice of Critical Teacher Leadership" by Jill Bradley-Levine, https://bit.ly/3NIDcnr

- How Educators Can Advocate for English Language Learners, All In! https://bit.ly/3XkL8yC

- *Ruthless Equity: Disrupt the Status Quo and Ensure Learning for ALL Students* by Ken Williams

Answers to Your Biggest Questions About Teaching Secondary Science

What Are Some Frequently Asked Questions From Secondary Science Teachers?

A collection of questions not covered explicitly elsewhere in the book that are typically asked by secondary science teachers follows.

SHOULD I INTERJECT CORRECT VOCABULARY WHEN STUDENTS ARE EXPLAINING IDEAS?

While there are many reasons to encourage students' correct use of vocabulary, one important reason is that using vocabulary specific to the discipline means students are able to speak the same language. When students use their own words to explain an idea, their reasoning must be interpreted by other students. As students become more familiar with the meaning of common words of the discipline, they can be more confident that they are communicating the ideas they want to their classmates. So we suggest allowing students to share their reasoning in their own words and then using scaffolds like word walls, sentence starters, or other discourse supports to help students connect their reasoning to disciplinary vocabulary.

WHERE CAN I FIND FUNDING FOR RESOURCES WHEN MY CLASSROOM OR DEPARTMENT DOESN'T HAVE WHAT I NEED?

Here are a few places where teachers can look to get materials for their classrooms:

- DonorsChoose, https://www.donorschoose.org/teachers
- STEM grants, https://stemfinity.com/pages/stem-grants
- Fund for Teachers, https://www.fundforteachers.org/
- The NEA Foundation, https://www.neafoundation.org/educator-grants-and-fellowships
- The National Science Teaching Association Awards, https://www.nsta.org/awards-and-recognition-program

For PBL funding, you can go to the following:

- Toshiba America Foundation, https://www.toshiba.com/taf/about.jsp

You can also apply for a teaching fellowship that comes with grant money. A couple of popular options are:

- the Knowles Teaching Fellowship, https://knowlesteachers.org/,
- the Institute for Citizens Scholars Fellowships, https://citizensandscholars.org/fellowships/all-fellowships/.

GROWTH

What Are Some Frequently Asked Questions From Secondary Science Teachers?

163

Companies and organizations sometimes will give you demonstration materials if you attend a session of theirs or if you ask for a donation. Also look into local organizations and partnerships in your area for grant money opportunities, such as university STEM programs and local art programs who want to fund STEAM teaching projects. Lastly, for more general supply donations, join your local Buy Nothing group on Facebook where you can ask for anything you might need and neighbors will freely give materials to you.

HOW DO I DEVELOP AND GAIN COMFORT WITH MY TEACHER IDENTITY?

It takes time: It's about consistency and trying new things. Relationship- and culture-building will help you gain comfort with your classroom and with yourself in your classroom. As you try new things and gain more experience, you will figure out what your teaching personality is like.

WHAT IS THE DIFFERENCE BETWEEN RULES AND NORMS?

Rules are explicit, nonnegotiable regulations presented by the teacher and/or school. They often determine dress code, phone use, or attendance policy. Norms are collective agreements for how students and teachers will build your classroom community with each other. While they serve different purposes, rules and norms work together to create a safe, productive learning environment.

WHAT DO I DO IF I'M REQUIRED TO FOLLOW A PACING GUIDE AND STUDENTS AREN'T LEARNING AS QUICKLY AS I WANT THEM TO?

It can be challenging to teach by a pacing guide that moves too quickly through the curriculum for your students. To address this challenge, consider incorporating investigations or projects that encompass multiple standards (see PBL Overview p. 86). This approach ensures that students don't learn content in isolation; instead, they simultaneously cover multiple concepts in a more integrated manner. You can also work with colleagues who are more familiar with the pacing guide to co-plan units or lessons to make sure that you are scaffolding lessons in ways that support the range of students you are teaching (see Unit Planning p. 56; Lesson Planning p. 60).

HOW DO I SUPPORT MY STUDENTS IN PERFORMING SUCCESSFULLY ON COMMON BENCHMARK ASSESSMENTS IN MY SCHOOL?

One way to support students is by clearly communicating the expectations and structures that students can expect to see on the assessment (types of questions, number of questions, time to take, etc.). Make sure that accommodations for students with individual education or 504 plans, or who are ESOL, are being met.

Practice the assessment conditions with students ahead of time and discuss successful strategies for taking the assessment.

HOW DO I SUPPORT STUDENTS WHO MISS A LOT OF INSTRUCTIONAL DAYS?

Although absences are out of your control, developing support structures for your classroom *is* squarely in your control. Communicate with caregivers, guidance counselors, administration, and other support staff, such as social workers and instructional coaches, to make sure that adults are aware and available to support students as needed. Be sure that all of the material you are teaching that students miss is readily accessible for them upon return or available electronically to complete when they are not at school. Direct instruction can be easily shared through the myriad of instructional videos on YouTube and readings on Khan Academy. Make sure that you preview each video or reading to make sure that it is appropriate for the grade level that you teach. Finally, consider whether students need an individualized plan to support them in getting caught up.

HOW DO I NAVIGATE UNSUPPORTIVE/ UNCOLLABORATIVE COLLEAGUES, ADMINISTRATION, ETC.?

It can be challenging when you feel unsupported by your colleagues at work. One way to approach this issue is to seek to learn from them before trying to change their classroom practice. Just like with students, building relationships with your colleagues can lead to building community in your department. Some ways to build relationships are to ask to visit colleagues' classrooms to see how they teach, inquire about students that they are especially good at teaching/reaching, and ask about why they started teaching.

WHAT ARE SOME WAYS TO PREPARE IF MY DISTRICT REQUIRES ME TO USE A TEXTBOOK IN MY TEACHING?

While there are many resources for great science-teaching curriculum, some schools or districts require teachers to use the adopted textbook. Before using your textbook in class, read the beginning of the teacher version to get a sense of the pedagogical perspective of the authors, see how the units are organized, and determine what opportunities there are for extensions.

HOW DO I BALANCE ADDITIONAL RESPONSIBILITIES AT WORK?

Prioritize saying yes to the responsibilities that are meaningful for you and no to those that are not. If a responsibility is mandatory, try and pair it with something positive, such as doing it with a work friend, working in a physical area that is your favorite, or pairing the responsibility with a healthy, good-tasting snack or drink.

What Are Some Frequently Asked Questions From Secondary Science Teachers?

165

IF MY DISTRICT HAS A TEACHER UNION, WHAT SHOULD I CONSIDER BEFORE JOINING?

First, get to know the union context of your state. Is it right-to-work or collective bargaining? Right-to-work laws let workers choose whether to join a labor union in the workplace. Other states require all employees to join a union since they all benefit from collective bargaining. Unions can provide legal protection and counsel, help you voice your concerns, offer discount programs/benefits and professional development, and, depending on your district/state they can give you power to change the terms and conditions of teacher contracts (bargaining power). Unions, however, cost money, and you might not agree with the organization's values or feel like you need its services. The two biggest national teachers' unions are the National Education Association (NEA) and the American Federation of Teachers (AFT).

SHOULD I FRIEND COLLEAGUES ON SOCIAL MEDIA OR EXCHANGE PERSONAL CELL NUMBERS?

Sometimes a school or district might have a policy on your social media conduct (such as friending/following) and collegial relationships. It is easier to start out with stricter boundaries and lessen these once you get more established and learn more about your colleagues. If exchanging numbers, it's important to clearly communicate boundaries on the content and timing of communication.

WHAT SHOULD I DO AT THE END OF THE SCHOOL YEAR?

Sometimes your school will mandate the end-of-year activities (such as testing/finals), but there are many times when there are extra days after finals/testing that can be difficult to plan for. This is a great opportunity to do investigations that you have not had time for, or to plan fun, community-building activities with your class. Discuss with your students what they would like to do and plan.

HOW DO I AVOID BURNOUT?

Psychologists have defined *burnout* in terms of chronic and heightened stress, sleeplessness, cynicism, and feelings of ineffectiveness and inadequacy (Tapp, 2019). While burnout may not be something that is wholly avoidable given personal factors, there are some strategies that may reduce the likelihood of experiencing it.

- See if your district provides free counseling as a part of your benefits package. You may find these resources through an employee assistance program (EAP).
- Reflect on the aspects of your work that are most challenging and implement some strategies for bounding your time on them. For example, you can set a 30-minute timer to plan a lesson using a lesson-planning template (see Lesson Planning p. 60), modify a colleague's completed lesson plan to work in your classroom (see Learn and Grow p. 154), or ask to meet with a colleague for 30 minutes to draft a lesson plan together.
- Build a habit of reflection over time so that you can easily make adjustments to your lessons during the school year.

- Remember that growth is the aim, not perfection. Writing down three positive events that have occurred in each classroom and one important area for growth can help you have a more balanced view of your classroom practice. Then return to the area for growth on a regular interval to record progress.
- Apply an asset-based view to your students and yourself (see Communications p. 28). Focus both on what is going well and on strengths that can be built upon to develop the classroom culture that you and your students want.
- Engage in activities with your cherished social groups. Take time to think about other areas where you experience success and bring those identities to your classroom.
- Focus on the parts of your work that you can control.

HOW DO I SUPPORT STUDENTS WHO ARE STRUGGLING AT HOME?

When a student shares with you about struggles they are having at home, it is important that you do not take sides. There is a lot of context to challenges that may be impacting your student's home life. Be a listener if you can. Encourage your students to take advantage of counseling services in your school. Be transparent with the student about what information you can keep in confidence and what you are required to report to other school staff members or their family. Come up with a way for your student to share with you if they need some flexibility in their classroom. Phrases such as "I need more care" or "I'm not feeling my best today" might work. Finally, offer any flexibility that you can with classroom routines or expectations on days when your student indicates they've had an especially challenging day or night at home.

WHERE DO I GO FOR SUPPORT AROUND CLASSROOM BEHAVIOR MANAGEMENT?

Classroom management is a challenging skill to perfect because different students and classroom configurations require different norms (see Norms p. 71). It is also true that classroom management is an extension of our own identity, so strategies that work for another teacher may not work for you. So you may choose to read books on classroom management, talk with teachers in your school about what approaches have worked for particular classes or shared students, or take virtual or in-person training on classroom management provided by your district or by other organizations (see Learn and Grow p. 154).

Great Resources

"One Teaching Habit That Will Save You Time, Increase Your Impact, and Buy Back a Bit of Your Summer," by Ayanna Perry, https://bit.ly/3XomAoh;

"Teaching & Being Rachetdemic," TEDx Talk by Christopher Emdin, https://bit.ly/3qQu9YC

Great Resources

- "The Warm Demander: An Equity Approach," by Matt Alexander, https://edut.to/3qWuXvl
- Classroom Management, https://bit.ly/3CIFXyV
- *Culturally Responsive Teaching and The Brain: Promoting Authentic Engagement and Rigor Among Culturally and Linguistically Diverse Students* by Zaretta Hamond

GROWTH

What Are Some Frequently Asked Questions From Secondary Science Teachers?

167

WHERE CAN I LEARN MORE ABOUT MY SCHOOL'S EMERGENCY PROCEDURES?

Schools should have training on their emergency procedures. You should also be able to ascertain what your emergency procedures are for different school events by reading the school handbook. Review these procedures quarterly so that during emergencies you feel comfortable and ready to support your students and ensure their safety.

WHERE DO I GO FOR SUPPORT TEACHING ANTI-BULLYING?

There have been many public campaigns over the years to counter bullying in schools. Some of them can be found at StompOutBullying.org, Nobully.org, and Stopbullying.gov. These websites can provide teachers with information about anti-bullying strategies. You can also speak to your school counselor and consult your school's handbook on bullying policy. Finally, do not ignore reports of bullying or acts of bullying that you observe. Follow your school's policy for notifying administration and families about bullying to protect your students.

HOW DO I KEEP UP WITH DEVELOPING TECHNOLOGY?

There are a few ways to keep up with changing technology. You can

- attend regional or national conferences to see what is on display in the exhibition halls,
- partner with educational technology companies to pilot their new items,
- attend tech training provided by your school and district.

Great Resources

Free virtual labs, https://engineeringtomorrow.org/labs/; Information about science technology, https://scitechdaily.com/; Science videos and lessons, https://bit.ly/42TU1QW.

WHY IS IT IMPORTANT TO CONNECT WITH OTHER SCIENCE TEACHERS IN MY DISTRICT?

Collaboration between teachers at the same grade level, at the same grade-level band (elementary, middle school, high school) and between grade-level bands is important. Teachers at each grade level, even if they are in different buildings, can share what they are doing so that students have similar experiences. Good ideas may be happening in one classroom that can also happen in others. K–12 teachers of science can meet during professional learning community time to see how ideas are built upon from grade to grade.

The Next Generation Science Standards and many other science standards are written so that there is a progression of ideas, a coherence that builds with ideas and skills applied across time. New and existing knowledge is linked to previous ideas, and teachers help students make connections so that they won't have fragmented knowledge.

When teachers meet and share what they are doing, they can see these progressions and give students a coherent science education. Without teachers making time for collaboration within grade bands and across K–12, it is very difficult for these progressions to happen with students.

What Are Some Frequently Asked Questions From Secondary Science Teachers?

169

GROWTH

REFERENCES

Alexander, M. (2016). *The warm demander: An equity approach.* Edutopia. https://edut.to/3qWuXvl

Allen, D., & Blythe, T. (2004). *The facilitator's book of questions: Resources for looking together at student and teacher work.* Teachers College Press.

Almarode, J., Fisher, D., Frey, N., & Hattie, J. (2018). *Visible learning for science, grades K–12: What works best to optimize student learning.* Corwin.

Archibald, G. (2016). *My life with cranes.* International Crane Foundation.

AusAntarctic Science TV. (2022). *Oases of life* [Video]. YouTube. https://www.youtube.com/watch?v=EIN30dHikQU

Ballenger, C. (2009). *Puzzling moments, teachable moments: Practicing teacher research in urban classrooms.* Teachers College Press.

Banilower, E. P. S., Weiss, I. R., Malzahn, K. A., Campbell, K. M., & Weiss, A. M. (2013). Report of the 2021 national survey of science and mathematics education. Chapel Hill, N.C.: Horizon Research Inc.

Barres, B. (2020). *The autobiography of a transgender scientist.* MIT Press.

Beauchamp, A., Kusnick, J., McCallum, R., & Hollander, J. (2011). *Success in science through dialogue, reading and writing.* University of California, Davis.

Bishop, R. S. (1990). Mirrors, windows, and sliding glass doors. *Perspectives, 6*(3), ix–xi.

Blackburn, M. V., Clark, C. T., Kenney, L. M., & Smith, J. M. (Eds.). (2009). *Acting out! Combating homophobia through teacher activism.* Teachers College Press.

Blackburn, M. V., Clark, C. T., & Schey, R. (2018). *Stepping up! Teachers advocating for sexual and gender diversity in schools.* Routledge.

Blackley, A. (2019). *8 things successful co-teachers do.* We Are Teachers. https://bit.ly/42X12R1

Blythe, T., Allen, D., & Powell, B. S. (2015). *Looking together at student work.* Teachers College Press.

Borasi, R. (1996). *Reconceiving mathematics instruction: A focus on errors.* Greenwood Publishing Group.

Bradley-Levine, J. (2018). Advocacy as a practice of critical teacher leadership. *International Journal of Teacher Leadership, 9*(1). https://files.eric.ed.gov/fulltext/EJ1182705.pdf

Brown, B. A. (2019). *Science in the city: Culturally relevant STEM education.* Harvard Education Press.

Bruner, J. S. (1960). *The process of education.* Harvard University Press.

Bryant, W. F. (2020). *A recipe for planning an NGSS storyline: Curiosity, persistence, reflection and a library of resources.* Kaleidoscope. https://knowlesteachers.org/kaleidoscope/a-recipe-for-planning-an-ngss-storyline-curiosity-persistence-reflection-and-a-library-of-resources

Burant, T., Christensen, L., Walters, S., & Salas, K. D. (Eds.). (2010). *The new teacher book: Finding purpose, balance, and hope during your first years in the classroom.* Rethinking Schools.

Butcher, K. R., Hudson M., & Runburg, M. (2018). Visualizations for deep learning: Using 3D models to promote scientific observation and reasoning during collaborative STEM inquiry. In R. Zheng (Ed.), *Strategies for deep learning with digital technology: Theories and practices in education* (pp. 111–135). Nova Science Publishers.

Butcher, K. R., Runburg M., & Altizer R. (2017). Dino lab: Designing and developing an educational game for critical thinking. In R. Zheng & M. K. Gardner (Eds.), *The handbook of research on serious games for educational applications* (pp. 115–148). IGI Global.

Butler-Wall, A., Cosier, K., Harper, R., Sapp, J., Sokolower, J., & Tempel, M. B. (Eds.). (2016). *Rethinking sexism, gender, and sexuality.* Rethinking Schools.

Cartier, J. L., Smith, M. S., Stein, M. K., & Ross, D. K. (2013). *5 practices for orchestrating productive task-based discussions in science.* National Council of Teachers of Mathematics.

Chapman, C., & Hyatt, C. H. (2011). *Critical conversations in co-teaching: A problem-solving approach.* Solution Tree Press.

Christensen, L., Karp, S., Peterson, B., & Yonamine, M. (2019). *The new teacher book: Finding purpose, balance, and hope during your first years in the classroom.* Rethinking Schools.

Colburn, A. (2016). *Learning science by doing science: 10 classic investigations reimagined to teach kids how science really works, grades 3–8.* Corwin.

Cook, J., Oreskes, N., Doran, P. T., Anderegg, W. R., Verheggen, B., Maibach, E. W., Carlton, J. S., Lewandowsky, S., Skuce, A. G., Green, S. A., Nuccitelli, D., Jacobs, P., Richardson, M., Winkler, B., Painting, R., & Rice, K. (2016). Consensus on consensus: A synthesis of consensus estimates on human-caused global warming. *Environmental Research Letters, 11*(4). https://iopscience.iop.org/article/10.1088/1748-9326/11/4/048002

Cooper, H., Robinson, J. C., & Patall, E. A. (2006). Does homework improve academic achievement? A synthesis of research, 1987–2003. *Review of Educational Research, 76*(1), 1–62. https://doi.org/10.3102/00346543076001001

Duncan, R. G., Krajcik, J., & Rivet, A. E. (Eds.). (2016). *Disciplinary core ideas: Reshaping teaching and learning.* NSTA.

Dybas, C. L. (2006). On a collision course: Ocean plankton and climate change. *BioScience, 56*(8), 642–646. https://doi.org/10.1641/0006-3568(2006)56[642:oaccop]2.0.co;2

Fausch, K. D. (2015). *For the love of rivers: A scientist's journey.* Oregon State University Press.

Fogler, H. S., LeBlanc, S. E., & Rizzo, B. R. (2008). *Strategies for creative problem solving.* Prentice Hall.

Frank, A. (2018). *Light of the stars: Alien worlds and the fate of Earth.* W. W. Norton and Company Independent Publishers.

Gonzalez, J. (2016). *How to write a syllabus.* Cult of Pedagogy. https://www.cultofpedagogy.com/course-syllabus-how-to/

Green, J. (2020). *Powerful ideas of science and how to teach them.* Routledge.

Gross, H. (2022). *5 tips for co-teaching.* National Education Association. https://bit.ly/3JsWJWz

Gutiérrez, R. (2015). *Risky business: Mathematics teachers using creative insubordination.* Annual meeting of the North American Chapter of the International Group for the Psychology of Mathematics Education, East Lansing, Michigan. https://files.eric.ed.gov/fulltext/ED584302.pdf

Hammond, Z. (2014). *Culturally responsive teaching and the brain: Promoting authentic engagement and rigor among culturally and linguistically diverse students.* Corwin.

Handley, G., Lebed, A., & Morling, B. (2021). Self-graded homework helps students learn and promotes accurate metacognition. *Scholarship of Teaching and Learning in Psychology.* https://doi.org/10.1037/stl0000287

Harrington, J. N. (2019). *Buzzing with questions: The inquisitive mind of Charles Henry Turner.* Illustrated by T. Taylor III. Calkins Creek.

Hiebert, J., & Grouws, D. A. (2007). The effects of classroom mathematics teaching on students' learning. *Second Handbook of Research on Mathematics Teaching and Learning, 1*(1), 371–404.

Hiebert, J., & Wearne, D. (1993). Instructional tasks, classroom discourse, and students' learning in second-grade arithmetic. *American Educational Research Journal, 30*(2), 393–425. https://doi.org/10.3102/00028312030002393

Holmes, N. G., Keep, B., & Wieman, C. E. (2020). Developing scientific decision making by structuring and supporting student agency. *Physical Review Physics Education Research, 16*(9). https://doi.org/10.1103/PhysRevPhysEducRes.16.010109

Horn, I. (2012). *Strength in numbers: Collaborative learning in secondary mathematics.* National Council of Teachers of Mathematics.

Howard, T. C. (2020). *7 culturally responsive teaching strategies and instructional practices.* Houghton Mifflin Harcourt. https://www.hmhco.com/blog/culturally-responsive-teaching-strategies-instruction-practices

Jackson, R. R., & Lambert, C. (2010). *How to support struggling students. Mastering the principles of great teaching series.* ASCD.

Jahren, H. (2016). *Lab girl.* Knopf.

Kang, S. H. (2016). Spaced repetition promotes efficient and effective learning: Policy implications for instruction. *Policy Insights From the Behavioral and Brain Sciences, 3*(1), 12–19.

Keating, J. (2017). *Shark lady: The true story of How Eugenie Clark became the ocean's most fearless scientist.* Illustrated by Marta Álvarez Miguéns. Sourcebooks, Inc.

Keeley, P. (2015). *Science formative assessment, volume 1: 75 practical strategies for linking assessment, instruction, and learning.* Corwin.

Keeley, P., & Eberle, F. (2005). *Uncovering student ideas in science: Another 25 formative assessment probes.* NSTA.

Keeley, P., & Tugel, J. (2019). *Science curriculum topic study: Bridging the gap between three-dimensional standards, research, and practice.* Corwin.

Keenan, H. (2021). Keep yourself alive: Welcoming the next generation of queer and trans educators. *Occasional Paper Series, 2021*(45), 12.

Keller, E. F. (1984). *A feeling for the organism, 10th anniversary edition: The life and work of Barbara McClintock.* Macmillan.

Kim, A. Y., Sinatra, G. M., & Seyranian, V. (2018). Developing a STEM identity among young women: A social identity perspective. *Review of Educational Research, 88*(4), 589–625.

Kimmerer, R. W. (2022). *Braiding sweetgrass: Indigenous wisdom, scientific knowledge, and the teaching of plants.* Zest Books.

Kohli, R. (2021). *Teachers of color: Resisting racism and reclaiming education.* Harvard Education Press.

Lanham, J. D. (2016). *The home place: Memoirs of a colored man's love affair with nature.* Milkweed Editions.

Lin, J., & Perry, A. D. (2022). Should groups set their own norms? Maybe not. *The Learning Forward Journal, 43*(1), 30–33. https://learningforward.org/journal/building-community-in-a-divided-world/should-groups-set-their-own-norms-maybe-not/

Lin-Siegler, X., Dweck, C. S., & Cohen, G. L. (2016). Instructional interventions that motivate classroom learning. *Journal of Educational Psychology, 108*(3), 295.

Love, B. L. (2019). *We want to do more than survive: Abolitionist teaching and the pursuit of educational freedom.* Beacon Press.

McGee, E. O. (2020). *Black, brown, bruised: How racialized STEM education stifles innovation.* Harvard Education Press.

Mensah, F. M. (March/April 2021). Culturally relevant and culturally responsive: Two theories of practice for science teaching. *Science and Children, 58*(4). https://www.nsta.org/science-and-children/science-and-children-marchapril-2021/culturally-relevant-and-culturally

Michaels, S., & O'Connor, C. (2012). *Talk science primer.* TERC.

Morehead, K., Dunlosky, J., & Rawson, K. A. (2019). How much mightier is the pen than the keyboard for note-taking? A replication and extension of Mueller and Oppenheimer (2014). *Educational Psychology Review, 31*(3), 753–780.

Mueller, P. A., & Oppenheimer, D. M. (2014). The pen is mightier than the keyboard: Advantages of longhand over laptop note taking. *Psychological Science, 25*(6), 1159–1168.

National Council of Teachers of Mathematics. (2014). *Principles to actions: Ensuring mathematical success for all.* NCTM.

National Research Council. (2012). *A framework for K–12 science education: Practices, crosscutting concepts, and core ideas.* National Academies Press.

NGSS Lead States. (2013). *Next Generation Science Standards: For states, by states.* National Academies Press.

Nordine, J., & Lee, O. (Eds.). (2021). *Crosscutting concepts: Strengthening science and engineering learning.* NSTA.

Nyugen, H. P. (2022). *How to create authentic writing opportunities in the science classroom.* Edutopia. https://www.edutopia.org/article/creating-authentic-writing-opportunities-science-classroom/

Oreskes, N., & Conway, E. (2010). *Merchants of doubt: How a handful of scientists obscured the truth on issues from tobacco smoke to global warming.* Bloomsbury Press.

Owens, B. (2022). Beauty and wonder of science boosts researchers' well-being. *Nature.* https://doi.org/10.1038/d41586-022-00762-8

Paris, D., & Alim, H. S., & Genishi, C. (Eds.). (2017). *Culturally sustaining pedagogies: Teaching and learning for justice in a changing world.* Teachers College Press.

Perry, A. (2022). *One teaching habit that will save you time, increase your impact, and buy back a bit of your summer.* Corwin Connect. https://corwin-connect.com/2022/04/one-teaching-habit-that-will-save-you-time-increase-your-impact-and-buy-back-a-bit-of-your-summer/

Reiser, B. (2016). *Designing coherent storylines aligned with NGSS for the K–12 classroom.* Academia. https://bit.ly/3GObKBx

Schleifer, D., Rinehart, C., & Yanisch, T. (2017). *Teacher collaboration in perspective: A guide to research.* https://files.eric.ed.gov/fulltext/ED591332.pdf

Schwarz, C. V., Passmore, C., & Reiser, B. J. (Eds.). (2017). *Helping students make sense of the world using next generation science and engineering practices.* NSTA.

Shetterly, M. L. (2016). *Hidden figures: The American Dream and the untold story of the Black women mathematicians who helped win the space race.* William Morrow.

Sriram, R. (2020, April 13). *The neuroscience behind productive struggle.* Edutopia. https://www.edutopia.org/article/neuroscience-behind-productive-struggle

Stenger, M. (2014). *5 research-based tips for providing students with meaningful feedback.* Edutopia. https://www.edutopia.org/blog/tips-providing-students-meaningful-feedback-marianne-stenger

Stipek, D. J., Givvin, K. B., Salmon, J. M., & MacGyvers, V. L. (2001). Teachers' beliefs and practices related to mathematics instruction. *Teaching and Teacher Education, 17*(2), 213–226.

Suarez, M. I., & Mangin, M. M. (Eds.). (2022). *Trans studies in K–12 education: Creating an agenda for research and practice.* Harvard Education Press.

Sztajn, P. (2003). Adapting reform ideas in different mathematics classrooms: Beliefs beyond mathematics. *Journal of Mathematics Teacher Education, 6*, 53–75.

Tapp, F. (2019). *Teacher burnout: Causes, symptoms, and prevention.* Hey Teach! https://www.wgu.edu/heyteach/article/teacher-burnout-causes-symptoms-and-prevention1711.html

Teach Engineering. (n.d.). *Next Generation Science Standards.* https://www.teachengineering.org/standards/ngss

Truong, D. (2022). Detracking in K–12 classrooms. *U.S. News & World Report.* https://bit.ly/3NoGavX

Watson, D., Hagopian, J., & Au, W. (Eds.). (2018). *Teaching for Black lives.* Rethinking Schools.

Wentzel, K. (2014). Commentary: The role of goals and values in critical-analytic thinking. *Educational Psychology Review, 26*(4), 579–582.

Wiggins, G. (2012, September 1). *Seven keys to effective feedback.* ASCD. https://www.ascd.org/el/articles/seven-keys-to-effective-feedback

Wilson, E. O. (1994). *Naturalist.* Island Press.

Windschitl, M., Thompson, J., & Braaten, M. (2020). *Ambitious science teaching.* Harvard Education Press.

Wirebring, L. K., Lithner, J., Jonsson, B., Liljekvist, Y., Norqvist, M., & Nyberg, L. (2015). Learning mathematics without a suggested solution method: Durable effects on performance and brain activity. *Trends in Neuroscience and Education, 4*(1–2), 6–14.

INDEX

Answers to Your Biggest Questions About Teaching Secondary Science

CORWIN Mathematics

Supporting TEACHERS | Empowering STUDENTS

PETER LILJEDAHL

14 optimal practices for thinking that create an ideal setting for deep mathematics learning to occur.
Grades K–12

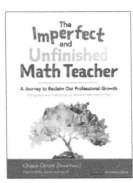

CHASE ORTON

A guide that leads math teachers through a journey to cultivate a more equitable, inclusive, and cohesive culture of professionalism for themselves.
Grades K–12

KIMBERLY RIMBEY

Much needed guidance on how to meet the diverse needs of students using small group math instruction.
Grades K–5

BETH MCCORD KOBETT, FRANCIS (SKIP) FENNELL, KAREN S. KARP, DELISE ANDREWS, LATRENDA KNIGHTEN, JEFF SHIH, DESIREE HARRISON, BARBARA ANN SWARTZ, SORSHA-MARIA T. MULROE

Detailed plans for helping elementary students experience deep mathematical learning.
Grades K–1, 2–3, 4–5

LOU EDWARD MATTHEWS, SHELLY M. JONES, YOLANDA A. PARKER

A resource for designing inspiring learning experiences driven by the kind of high-quality and culturally relevant mathematics tasks that connect students to their world.
Elementary, Middle and High School

JOHN J. SANGIOVANNI, SUSIE KATT, KEVIN J. DYKEMA

A guide for empowering students to embrace productive struggle to build essential skills for learning and living—both inside and outside the classroom.
Grades K–12

To order, visit corwin.com/math

**JENNIFER M. BAY-WILLIAMS,
JOHN J. SANGIOVANNI,
ROSALBA SERRANO,
SHERRI MARTINIE,
JENNIFER SUH, C. DAVID WALTERS**

Because fluency is so much more
than basic facts and algorithms.
Grades K–8

**ROBERT Q. BERRY III, BASIL M. CONWAY IV,
BRIAN R. LAWLER, JOHN W. STALEY,
COURTNEY KOESTLER, JENNIFER WARD,
MARIA DEL ROSARIO ZAVALA,
TONYA GAU BARTELL, CATHERY YEH,
MATHEW FELTON-KOESTLER,
LATEEFAH ID-DEEN,
MARY CANDACE RAYGOZA,
AMANDA RUIZ, EVA THANHEISER**

Learn to plan instruction that engages
students in mathematics explorations
through age-appropriate and culturally
relevant social justice topics.
**Early Elementary, Upper Elementary,
Middle School, High School**

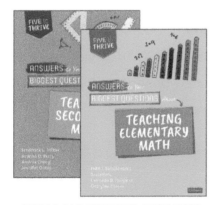

**JOHN J. SANGIOVANNI, SUSIE KATT,
LATRENDA D. KNIGHTEN,
GEORGINA RIVERA,
FREDERICK L. DILLON,
AYANNA D. PERRY,
ANDREA CHENG, JENNIFER OUTZS**

Actionable answers to your most
pressing questions about teaching
elementary and secondary math.
Elementary, Secondary

**SARA DELANO MOORE,
KIMBERLY RIMBEY**

A journey toward making
manipulatives meaningful.
Grades K–3, 4–8

CM22153268

Helping educators make the greatest impact

CORWIN HAS ONE MISSION: to enhance education through intentional professional learning.

We build long-term relationships with our authors, educators, clients, and associations who partner with us to develop and continuously improve the best evidence-based practices that establish and support lifelong learning.